AN ILLUSTRATED GUIDE TO
DOGS

MARGARET KEENAN

Published in 2009 by TAJ Books International LLP

27, Ferndown Gardens,
Cobham,
Surrey,
UK,
KT11 2BH

www.tajbooks.com

ISBN-13: 978-1-84406-139-6

Printed in China.

AN ILLUSTRATED GUIDE TO
DOGS

MARGARET KEENAN

T&J

INTRODUCTION

The most popular non-human companion round the world is the dog, a faithful, loyal, friendly, and useful member of the family. Dogs far more than any other animal (with the arguable exception of the horse, but they don't share our hearth and home) have helped people to earn a living and fight for life. Without dogs our early ancestors would have struggled to hunt as successfully and herd their animals as safely.

Of course there are still many working dogs today, but their usefulness is an exception rather than a rule—sheepdogs and police dogs are the commonest examples of animals that are esteemed for their intelligence and working prowess. One of the most valuable roles for our canine friends is as seeing dogs, guiding their blind owners safely around. These exceptionally clever and able dogs are, literally, a lifeline for their owners, not only guiding and protecting their handler but also providing incomparable companionship. In fact the latter is the role most often fulfilled by dogs in the modern world; the sense of protection and security is valuable, but dogs are most loved for their company and affection. Most dogs are more than willing to utterly adore their owner and family and are willing to overlook almost any setback just as long as they are spoken to, loved, and fed. Many dogs take their cue from their handler with regard to their temperament: a dog that is loved and well looked after is more than likely to be open and affectionate, whereas it is no surprise if a mistreated dog is surly and aggressive if it has never been treated with care. Indeed, it is often said that dogs and their owners look much the same and while this is a wild exaggeration, nevertheless it is amusing to note how often they will share similar characteristics. It really does seem more often than coincidence that owners with shaggy hair prefer dogs with shaggy coats, neat and tidy people seem to prefer neat and tidy dogs, and ladies who lunch invariably prefer small but perfectly formed (expensive) miniature dogs!

Almost all dog types were developed for a particular purpose and became specialized for that particular task. Consequently, hunting dogs possess enormous stamina; retrievers are valued for their "soft" mouth that does not damage fallen prey shot down by the hunter; dachshunds are long and wiry for wriggling down badger holes; greyhounds are built for speed; bloodhounds for their incredible sense of smell; and so on. Each breed has its own advocates—the choice is so personal and is invariably based on previous experience.

All dog breeds hail back to the distant past when they were of mixed wolf and, possibly, wild dog ancestry. Then, over the years, specific attributes were bred through deliberate crossing of existing breeds as well as through random chance. Breeders deliberately manipulated their dogs by encouraging desirable traits and spurning animals with non-desirable characteristics. Once the desired shape and color was achieved, the desired characteristics were maintained across succeeding generations through careful breeding. This type of breeding has to be carefully controlled or genetic disorders can become so pronounced that they can become detrimental to the dog's health. For example, German Shepherds are notorious for hip dysphasia, and Bulldogs can be so interbred that they frequently suffer from breathing problems.

The huge range of size, color, shape, and temperament of dogs is due to deliberate human selection of animals for specific functions.

History of the Dog

Mankind and dogs have shared their lives for at least 15,000 years and the fossil record indicates that this may in fact date as far back as 100,000 years. The Latin for dog is *Canis lupus familiaris* and references the fact that dogs were domesticated and bred from wolves; whether this was directly or via wolves and wild dogs interbreeding is debatable. As with so much from prehistory, the origin of dogs is greatly contested by experts. Some theorize that dogs were first domesticated in deepest Asia. As proof they cite that genetic research shows many of the most ancient breeds come from China and Japan—the Akita Inu, Basenji, Chow Chow, Shar Pei, and Shiba Inu, to name the best known.

From Asia dogs accompanied human migrants across the continent to Europe, Africa, and North America. As the dogs were assigned special tasks—herding and protecting being the principal jobs—the animals became more specialized, for climate, altitude, temperature, and so on. It would not have taken early man long to realize the advantages that hunting dogs would bring to their lives and the extra food to the table. Reciprocally, the dogs would have been rewarded with food and shelter and so the bonds between humans and canines would have strengthened and developed. Selective breeding emphasized and exaggerated certain characteristics and over time distinct breeds emerged. The greatest diversity within dogs, however, was from the genetic makeup of the ancestral wolves, that differed greatly between the subspecies.

Wolves in warm climate areas would have had short, light pelts and so were the ancestors of the short-haired breeds. Conversely, the long-haired, northern wolves are the ancestors of the longer-haired varieties of dog. Furthermore, when one factors in thousands of years and generations, selective breeding, natural adaptation, survival of the fittest, and human intervention—all the great range and diversity of dogs becomes more obvious. No wonder a dog can be anything from a Chihuahua to a St. Bernard. Although some of the most ancient dog breeds are still extant, most of the pedigree breeds are relatively recent developments, and these have derived from selective breeding programs that have resulted in significant differences between dogs with some types being highly specific for their purpose—for example, bloodhounds.

Wolves are members of the species *Canis lupus* and in ancient times they were split into a number of different subspecies such as the Indian wolf, the Japanese wolf, the Chinese wolf, the European wolf, and the Eastern Timber wolf. Each of these contributed different traits and attributes to the gene pool mix that became *Canis lupus familiaris*. The European wolf is the distant ancestor to many of the terriers and sheepdogs as well as to the strong, thick-pelted Spitz dog types. Together with the Indian Wolf, the European is thought to create the mastiffs, as well as the St. Bernard, bloodhounds, and pugs.

The Chinese wolf is the distant ancestor of toy spaniels and, unsurprisingly, the Pekinese; also, together with the European wolf, it is probably the progenitor of many of the oriental toy breeds. Most North American sled dogs are descended from the Eastern Timber wolf that handed down their immense strength, endurance, aggression, and ability to withstand extremely low temperatures. Indeed, this interbreeding still occurs in the Arctic regions with the result that it is not always entirely clear whether an animal is mostly wolf or primarily dog—the point anyway being largely academic in such extreme environments.

Given the loyal, amenable, and playful nature of dogs they would have quickly moved directly into the human living areas, and rather than just being used as guard dogs, would have quickly become valuable companions as well. Furthermore, their ingrained pack animal instincts would have helped them to assimilate into family groups with ease. This had many advantages for the dogs, not least that in most places it became taboo to eat dog, so ensuring the animals' safety even in times of famine. Research into the domestication of the dog continues and the latest thought is that a wild dog could have been domesticated using deliberate selective breeding through the course of two human generations. This is remarkably rapid in evolutionary terms but explicable when the best interests of both sides are recognized. The wild dogs would have received more food, warmth, and comfort if they were friendly and approachable to humans; hostile and aggressive dogs were more likely to be killed or driven away. For the humans the advantages were less immediately obvious until the dogs were amenable enough to help with the hunting. Meanwhile guard animals would raise the alarm should strangers or hostile animals appear near camp, and would be useful for clearing up edible leftovers that would otherwise rot and attract flies or predators to the settlement.

American Kennel Club

Pedigree dogs all have one inherent problem: they are descended from (in a historical time frame) a limited gene pool. With the more popular and populous breeds this is easily overcome by selecting mates from distant bloodlines. But when a breed is rare this option is not always possible and careless (or unlucky) breeding can lead to incurable genetic problems that can hamper the health of the dog, distort its behavior, and even shorten its life. Responsible breeders now use DNA testing, health reports, and careful selection of bloodlines before breeding their animals. One of the advantages of careful pure breeding is that the appearance, temperament, and behavior of the animal can be predicted with almost total certainty.

The largest official regulating body looking after the interests of pure-bred dogs in America is the American Kennel Club (AKC). The club keeps a pedigree registry for all recognized breeds and organizes various dog-related events and shows across the United States. The two premier events are the annual Westminster Kennel Club Dog Show and the American Kennel Club/Eukanuba National Championship. To be registered (and officially recognized) a puppy's parents must be registered with the AKC as belonging to the same breed, and the litter has to be registered. All that registration shows is that a dog officially belongs to a named breed: it does not concern itself with purity of blood or healthy ancestors. Most dog owners do not need to register their pets: it is only necessary for breeders who are in the business of selling puppies and for people who want to show their animals.

Dog shows are the highlight of many a breeder's calendar as this is the chance to show off their beloved animals. When it comes to showing, each breed has their physical characteristics judged against a single breed standard that is drawn up an adjudicated as the national standard. In the United States the arbiter of this is the American Kennel Club. The AKC oversees the pedigree and registration of dogs across America and also decrees the breed standards that individual dogs must achieve for top breeding and showing purposes.

AKC official groups

The AKC recognizes eight different dog types—and although other national canine organizations recognize some different breeds, the international organizations broadly agree on the same breeds with some local differences. For example, the AKC recognizes the American water spaniel as a distinct pedigree breed, but it is not recognized by the official kennel clubs in the United Kingdom, Australia, or New Zealand.

The AKC orders the various dog breeds into seven distinct groups, plus one class, and the Foundation Stock Service. These are:

- the Sporting Group, that contains twenty-six breeds
- the Hound Group with twenty-two breeds
- the Working Group with twenty-four breeds
- the Terrier Group with twenty-seven breeds
- the Toy Group with twenty-one breeds
- the Non-Sporting Group with seventeen breeds
- the Herding Group with eighteen breeds
- the the Miscellaneous Class with six breeds

The Sporting Group (aka Gundog Group)

These dogs are all closely associated with hunting and shooting and are used in field sports to flush out and then retrieve the prey. Accordingly, these dogs tend to be on the large side, require plenty of outdoor exercise, and are often marked by their gregarious nature and liveliness. The list of twenty-six breeds includes some of the most popular breeds of all, in particular ten different types of spaniel—the American Water Spaniel, American Cocker Spaniel, Clumber Spaniel, English Cocker Spaniel, English Springer Spaniel, Field Spaniel, French Spaniel, Irish Water Spaniel, Sussex Spaniel, and the Welsh Springer Spaniel—and six different types of retriever, namely the Chesapeake

Bay Retriever, Curly Coated Retriever, Flat-Coated Retriever, Golden Retriever, Labrador Retriever, and the Nova Scotia Duck-Tolling Retriever. Other members of this group include the setters—English Setter, Gordon Setter, Irish Red and White Setter, and the Irish Setter; the pointers—German Longhaired Pointer, German Shorthaired Pointer, German Wirehaired Pointer, and the Pointer. The others in this group are the Barbet, Bracco Italiano, Braque du Bourbonnais, Brittany, Cesky Fousek, Drentse Patrijshond, Kooikerhondje, Lagotto Romagnolo, Large Münsterländer, Small Münsterländer, Spanish Water Dog, Spinone Italiano, Vizsla, and last but not least, the Weimaraner.

The Hound Group

This group comprises a wide range and type of hunting dogs that are prized for their stamina—needed in the search for, pursuit, and running down of prey—and acute sense of smell. Many of them are long-legged and built for speed and were the prized hunting dogs of kings and nobles. The group comprises fifteen different kinds of hound: the Afghan Hound, American Foxhound, Basset Hound, Black and Tan Coonhound, Bloodhound, Dachshund, English Foxhound, Greyhound, Ibizan Hound, Irish Wolfhound, Norwegian Elkhound, Otterhound, Pharaoh Hound, Plott Hound, and the Scottish Deerhound. Others in the group are the Basenji, Beagle, Borzoi, Harrier, Petit Basset Griffon Vendéen, Rhodesian Ridgeback, Saluki, and the Whippet.

The Working Group

 In the past more than in the present, these dogs have been crucial to human survival. They are usually large and companionable dogs that enjoy working in close contact with their master but are not normally recommended as family pets; indeed, some of them fall into the "one person dog" category—this is particularly true of some of the sheepdogs. Additionally their greater intelligence than most other types of dog means that they need constant stimulation in the form of challenging work. Some of these breeds are traditionally used as guard dogs and when trained in this way need to be approached with great caution and circumspection. In alphabetical order they are: the Akita, Alaskan Malamute, Anatolian Shepherd Dog, Bernese Mountain Dog, Black Russian Terrier, Boxer, Bullmastiff, Doberman Pinscher, German Pinscher, Giant Schnauzer, Great Dane, Great Pyrenees (aka Pyrenean Mountain Dog), Greater Swiss Mountain Dog, Komondor,

Kuvasz, Mastiff, Neapolitan Mastiff, Newfoundland, Portuguese Water Dog, Rottweiler, Saint Bernard, Samoyed, Siberian Husky, Standard Schnauzer, and the Tibetan Mastiff.

The Terrier Group

This group contains many popular dogs that are often noted for their spirit and sometimes overt aggression. They were mostly bred originally as hunter-killers; in other words, they would be trained to find and then kill smaller animals such as rabbits, squirrels, rats, foxes, and even for baiting badgers. The AKC allocates one non-terrier breed, the Schnauzer (Miniature), in this category because it is similar in character and bred for the same purposes as terriers. Other kennel clubs do not concur with this classification. In alphabetical order the terriers are: the Airedale Terrier, American Pit Bull Terrier, American Staffordshire Terrier, Australian Terrier, Border Terrier, Bull Terrier, and Bull Terrier (Miniature), Cairn Terrier, Cesky Terrier, Dandie Dinmont Terrier, Fox Terrier (Smooth), Fox Terrier (Wire), Glen of Imaal Terrier, Irish Terrier, Jack Russell Terrier, Kerry Blue Terrier, Lakeland Terrier, Manchester Terrier, Norfolk Terrier, Norwich Terrier, Parson Russell Terrier, Schnauzer (Miniature), Scottish Terrier, Sealyham Terrier, Skye Terrier, Soft Coated Wheaten Terrier, Staffordshire Bull Terrier, Tenterfield Terrier, Welsh Terrier, and West Highland White Terrier

The Toy Group

These breeds are collectively the smallest pedigree dogs and are popular with their owners as possessing all the qualities of their bigger relatives without the size! This group includes five more breeds of terrier: the Australian Silky Terrier, English Toy Terrier (Black and Tan), Manchester Terrier, Toy Fox Terrier, and the Yorkshire Terrier. There are three kinds of spaniel—the Cavalier King Charles Spaniel, the King Charles Spaniel, and the Tibetan Spaniel. The remainder of this group includes the Affenpinscher, Belgian Griffon, Bolognese, Brussels Griffon, Chihuahua, Chinese Crested, Coton de Tulear, Havanese, Italian Greyhound, Japanese Chin, Kromfohrlander, Löwchen, Maltese, Miniature Pinscher, Miniature Poodle, Papillon, Pekingese, Peruvian Inca Orchid, Petit Brabancon, Pomeranian, Pug, and the Shih Tzu.

The Non-Sporting Group or Companion Group

Some of these breeds previously belonged in the Toy Group. The group consists of a small and diverse grouping of dogs that do not fit comfortably into any other category. These are animals such as the American Eskimo Dog, Bichon Frise, Boston Terrier, Bulldog, Chinese Shar-Pei, Chow Chow, Dalmatian, Finnish Spitz, French Bulldog, Keeshond, Lhasa Apso, Schipperke, Shiba Inu, Tibetan Spaniel, Tibetan Terrier, and the Toy Poodle.

The Herding Group

This group had its name changed in 1983 from the Working Group as the new name more accurately reflects the purpose of these breeds: herding and guarding livestock. These are intelligent animals that require a lot of stimulation and exercise;, they love company and make good family dogs. This small but select group includes: the Australian Cattle Dog, Australian Shepherd, Bearded Collie, Belgian Malinois, Belgian Sheepdog, Belgian Tervuren, Border Collie, Bouvier des Flandres, Briard, Canaan Dog, Cardigan Welsh Corgi, Collie, German Shepherd Dog, Old English Sheepdog, Pembroke Welsh Corgi, Polish Lowland Sheepdog, Puli, and the Shetland Sheepdog.

The Miscellaneous Class

There are only six breeds of dog in this category, and none of them is an officially recognized breed as yet. This could change if and when the breeds become widely enough supported by breeding programs. This exclusive listing contains the Beauceron, Dogue de Bordeaux, Plott, Redbone Coonhound, Swedish Vallhund, and the Tibetan Mastiff.

The Foundation Stock Service

The final grouping named by the AKC is the list of dogs on the Foundation Stock Service. These are rare breeds whose owners are hoping to establish the breed in the U.S. This occurs when and if a minimum of 150 dogs are registered with the AKC, at which point the breed concerned will be allowed to join in some of the AKC's competitions. The breeds working toward recognition include five of the Miscellaneous Class (Beauceron, Dogue de Bordeaux, Plott, Redbone Coonhound, Swedish Vallhund) as well as the American English Coonhound, Appenzeller Sennenhund, Argentine Dogo, Azawakh, Belgian Laekenois, Bergamasco, Black and Tan Coonhound, Bluetick Coonhound, Bolognese, Boykin Spaniel,

Bracco Italiano, Cane Corso, Catahoula Leopard Dog, Caucasian Mountain Dog, Central Asian Shepherd Dog, Cesky Terrier, Chinook, Coton de Tulear, Czechoslovakian Wolfdog, Entlebucher Mountain Dog, Estrela Mountain Dog, Finnish Lapphund, German Spitz, Grand Basset Griffon Vendéen, Icelandic Sheepdog, Irish Red and White Setter, Kai Ken, Karelian Bear Dog, Kishu Ken, Kooikerhondje, Lagotto Romagnolo, Lancashire Heeler, Leonberger, Mudi, Norwegian Buhund, Norwegian Lundehund, Perro de Presa Canario, Peruvian Inca Orchid, Portuguese Podengo, Portuguese Pointer, Pumi, Pyrenean Shepherd, Rafeiro do Alentejo, Rat Terrier, Russell Terrier, Schapendoes, Sloughi, Small Munsterlander Pointer, South African Boerboel, Spanish Water Dog, Stabyhoun, Thai Ridgeback, Tosa, Treeing Tennessee Brindle, Treeing Walker Coonhound, and the Xoloitzcuintli.

Top Ten Most Popular Breeds

Despite such an extensive choice of pedigree dog breeds the same breeds are perennially popular with the American public, year in, year out.

Labrador Retriever

The most popular and extensively owned breed recorded and registered in recent years with the American Kennel Club remains the Labrador Retriever, for which in 2006 there were 123,760 AKC recorded dogs. Familiar to everyone, Labradors are predominantly either black or golden, and less often, chocolate. They possess long, strong tails that wag very readily and knock over pretty much everything within reach. Labradors are sturdy, medium-sized dogs that were originally gun dogs used for retrieving shot birds or rabbits; accordingly they have very "soft" mouths. Huntsmen still predominantly use labradors when wildfowling. They are friendly, gregarious dogs and make great family pets provided that they get sufficient exercise to prevent them getting fat—a tendency they are prone to. They have a short, weather-resistant coat that repels water well, a useful trait as they are incorrigible when it comes to water, which they adore and will jump into without the slightest excuse.

Yorkshire Terrier

A long way numerically behind, yet still the second most popular pedigree dog in the U.S with 48,346 recorded dogs in 2006 is the Yorkshire Terrier. "Yorkies," as they are affectionately known, are small, silky-coated, naturally long-haired dogs. Their steel-blue and tan coat is pale at the front and dark over most of their body, and non-show animals usually have their coats shorn for convenience. Yorkies are known for their feisty manner, which is in complete contrast to their small size. Due to their stature they can easily be picked up in one hand and tucked under an arm. They are ideal dogs to have when space is limited.

German Shepherd Dog

Alsatians have dropped to third most popular place with 43,575 recorded dogs in the U.S. in 2006. These are large, powerful, and intelligent dogs frequently used for law-enforcement purposes; generally speaking, they are not ideal family dogs as they require more stimulation and exercise than most families provide. Those that are family dogs will guard the house and family members with absolute determination and authority. Most German Shepherds are medium-haired with a black and tan coat, although less often they can be long-haired and single-colored. They present a very distinctive silhouette finished off with a long, scimitar-curved tail.

Golden Retriever

In fourth place is the Golden Retriever with 42,962 registered animals. Similar in many ways—not least temperament and size—to the Labrador Retriever, the biggest difference to the layman is in their length of coat which is longer and silkier than its cousin and always golden. They are large sporting dogs characterized by their eager, friendly, and confident nature.

Beagle

The Beagle occupies fifth place with 39,484 registered dogs. Originally pack hunting dogs, they are medium-sized and very affable animals that are especially happy in a family situation. They possess a medium-length, close, hard coat in shades of tan and brown or black, plus a characteristic white muzzle, chest, and legs. They carry their tail high and always look alert and eager to please.

Dachshund

The sixth most popular pedigree dog in America is the "Sausage Dog."

Very distinctive with their long bodies on short legs, Dachshunds are originally German hunting dogs bred for searching out rats, rabbits, and badgers. They come in either standard or miniature size and with three different types of coat: smooth, wire-haired, and long-haired in colors of tan, brown, and black. They are intelligent and frequently feisty little dogs with a great deal of character. If they get overweight they can have problems with their exceptionally long back, so it is particularly essential not to spoil them with treats—no matter what they may tell you.

Boxer

The Boxer comes in at number seven and is a medium-sized, strongly built animal with a powerfully alert and muscular look. Despite this appearance, Boxers are often most affectionate and friendly in nature and can make great family pets. Their short, shiny coat is fawn and brindle with white front and lower legs making them low maintenance in terms of grooming, they do require plenty of exercise though.

Poodles

America's eighth most popular breed, Poodles come in a wide range of shapes, sizes, and color. These active, intelligent dogs are often mistaken for being not much more than fashion victims for their extremely showy "poodle cut" coats—but that is the owner's choice, not the dog's. A standard Poodle is a large dog while a Miniature or Toy Poodle is tiny. Their densely textured, curly coat can be anything from white to cream, apricot, all shades of brown, to silver, gray, and black. No matter what their shade or size, Poodles are very "showy," elegant dogs.

Shih Tzu

This tiny animal is the ninth most registered dog in the U.S. in 2006. Once a Chinese imperial dog, Shih Tzus are tiny, alert, and lively with an arrogant carriage and confident gait. In spite of their small size and delicate appearance, they are a solid little breed. The naturally long coat is silky and flowing and generally comes in a melange of browns, cream or white; but whatever the color, Shih Tzus require constant attention to grooming. Happily they are affectionate and friendly little animals that like nothing more than close human company.

Miniature Schnauzer

In tenth place is the Miniature Schnauzer, a medium to small-sized dog that belongs to the Terrier Group. Although it is not really a terrier, it does share a number of the terrier's characteristics: it is alert and active with a propensity to aggression when provoked. Its short, wiry hard coat is salt and pepper colored, although black and silver and solid black are also available.

Crossbreeds

There are some 800 or so recognized dog breeds around the world and many different types of mixed-breed. In fact the vast majority of dogs belong to no recognized breed and have mixed parentage: these are generally referred to as mutts, mongrels, or crossbreeds. Any dog breed can successfully mate with another breed, the only constraints being too much difference in size. The resulting offspring can, in theory, be of any size, shape, coat, or color. However, extreme breed characteristics, such as the flat faces of boxers, often disappear even within one generation of crossbreeding.

In terminology a crossbred or hybrid animal is the (usually) deliberate breeding between two distinct types of dog. On the other hand a mongrel is the result of unknown mixed parentage.

When this indiscriminate mixing of breeds goes back a number of generations, as it often does, the resultant dog reverts to the generic type. That is they are of medium size, around 15–23 inches at the shoulder, weigh around 40 pounds, and have a shortish coat that is typically black or light brown. Recessive genes can produce an animal completely unlike the parents. This also reduces the chances of genetic disorders, a common problem in pure-bred animals that are often mated within a limited gene pool—so this generally makes for a healthier, more vigorous dog: a characteristic known as hybrid vigor. Crossbreed dogs are often noted for their intelligence and their willingness to learn new things. Crossbreeds on average live a longer and healthier life than pedigree dogs.

In the last few years it has become fashionable to cross certain breeds together to get a dog that looks a particular way—the derisively named "Designer Dogs." The Poodle is especially popular for use in this way. Known examples of popular crosses include the Cockapoo—a cross between a Poodle and a Cocker Spaniel, and the Labradoodle, a mix between a Labrador Retriever and a Poodle. A Peekapoo is a cross between a Pekingese and a Poodle; a Goldendoodle is a Poodle and a Golden Retriever; while a Dorgie is a cross between a Corgie and a Dachshund. A Pom-chi is a cross between a Chihuahua and a Pomeranian, and a Sprocker is a cross between an English Springer Spaniel and a Cocker Spaniel. There are many more such examples of hybrids. Such crosses do not automatically produce the benefits of both breeds: the unlucky recipient could inherit all the defects such as bad behavioral problems and genetic disorders. Nothing is guaranteed; however, such mixing and matching of breeds is how different breeds emerged in the first place.

Cynics suggest that such cross-bred dogs are made as much for the amusement of the name as for the animal itself. The hybrids are not recognized or endorsed by the major kennel clubs and associations around the world. Proponents say that their aim is to produce healthly dogs with good temperaments so as to be ideal domestic companions or pets; the given example is the Labradoodle which initially was bred as a guide dog for visually impaired people who suffered from allergies.

Working Dogs

Sheep Dogs

Other than for hunting purposes, historically the greatest use for dogs has been for herding and protecting animals: almost every country has its own indigenous breed for the purpose. They tend to the large side but in fact vary enormously in size, shape, weight, coat, and color. The characteristics they do share are intelligence and boundless energy, two virtues that make them ideal herding dogs but demanding domestic pets. Many of these dogs are highly specialized for looking after one particular type of animal.

Different dogs have different techniques for herding their animals, the most common of which are sheep, cattle, or reindeer. Perhaps the best-known sheepdog is the Border Collie which is worked and directed by the shepherd through the use of whistle or voice. They are most effective when working in pairs with one running behind the herd to move them forward and the other positioned in front to cut off any stray movement in the wrong direction. They are known to stare down the animals and move them as much by intimidation as movement. Other dogs such as the Welsh Corgi and Australian Cattle Dog are known as "heelers" because they nip at the heels of the animals they

are moving. Yet another method is employed by the Australian Koolie (a breed unrecognized by any kennel club). In addition to the other methods of control, these also jump onto the back of their animals. This technique is particularly effective in a crowded pen or stock yard.

The dogs that "head" move to the front or head of the stock to push them back towards the herder; those that "heel" move the stock by nipping the heels of the stock; the ones that "drive" move the herd forward from behind; while those that "cast" move out and around the herd; and a very few dogs "back" when they literally jump onto the backs of their charges to move them around.

Ultimately all herding characteristics are modified predatory behavior, and can be seen even in pedigree dogs who are generations away from their working ancestors. Sheepdogs when kept as family pets often attempt to herd and drive their human family when out together on excursions.

Police Dogs

These animals help law enforcement officers with a number of different aspects of their job; capture and detention of suspects, searching for suspects, and searching for hidden drugs or explosives. The dog handling divisions of police forces across the world are often popular jobs, not least for the close companionship of the dogs themselves. By far the most commonly used breed for both police and military work is the German Shepherd.

By the very nature of their work police dogs have to be extremely well disciplined and often form a particularly close bond with their handlers: together, they form an inseparable team. Many of them live with the handler and their family and so also have a social aspect to their lives and therefore also their behavior.

Police forces around the world use their dogs and dog handlers for a number of situations but especially for searching duties. Dogs are particularly valuable for tracking and looking for missing people or felons and can be especially useful when searching for drugs or explosives—something their highly sensitive sense of smell is remarkably effective at detecting. The United States Transportation Security Administration is responsible for the safety of seventy-five airports and thirteen major transit systems; in early 2007 they used 420 trained (mostly) German Shepherds on regular patrols around those compounds.

Elsewhere in airports around the world the Beagle is used to sniff baggage; they have superb noses and are said to alarm passengers less because of their friendly and unthreatening nature. The United States Department of Agriculture uses the Beagle Brigade as sniffer dogs for searching out illegal food items hidden in luggage being brought into the U.S. These Beagles wear a distinctive green jacket; their counterparts across the Pacific working for the Australian Quarantine and Inspection Service wear maroon jackets. Beagles are also used as sniffer dogs by the Ministry of Agriculture and Fisheries in New Zealand. Meanwhile in the United Kingdom Springer Spaniels have been used with great success to search for drugs and explosives.

Of course the best-known tracker is the Bloodhound (also occasionally known as the St. Hubert Hound), a dog with a highly developed sense of smell. Dogs like these are unparalleled in their ability to discover earthquake victims who have been covered with rubble and debris; and of course such dogs can more safely traverse dangerously unstable ground in their search for people.

Mountain Rescue Dogs

The most famous breed of rescue dog is the huge and friendly St. Bernard, a mountain breed that originated in the Swiss Alps. They are reckoned to be the largest and heaviest dog breed in the world but are truly gentle giants. The breed was originally a Swiss herding dog but became legendary and named for the treacherous Great St. Bernard Pass in the Western Alps between Italy and Switzerland. An order of monks live in a monastery there. They run a traveler's hospice named after Bernard of Menthon, a monk who established the resting post in the eleventh century, to help travelers along their way—and perhaps more importantly, to find and rescue them when they were lost. The earliest record of St. Bernard dogs helping to rescue lost travelers goes back to the seventeenth century.

The most celebrated St. Bernard was Barry, who lived at the monastery from 1800 to 1814. He is credited with saving anything from between forty and a hundred lives from the dangerous mountain snows and avalanches. Such was his reputation that his body is stuffed and mounted in the main entrance of the Natural History Museum in Berne.

I want a dog — but should I get one?

Owning a dog is a serious undertaking and should not be taken on in a whim; a dog is a companion for life and, all being well, will share your home for many happy years. Your lifestyle has to be compatible with a dog's needs or it is best not to become an owner. A dog needs affection and attention as well as food and water, and, depending on the breed, a lot of exercise. This last element has to be factored into your life—a dog has to be taken for a good walk every day or at worst every other day: if this is not compatible with your lifestyle then a dog is not for you.

Similarly, although a dog can be left alone for short periods it is not fair to the animal to be abandoned every day while its master goes to work. The dog will pine and may well become uncommunicative and quite possibly destructive if left to its own devices for long periods. Furthermore the animal can bark incessantly if left alone, unfair to the dog and an aural nuisance for all neighbors within earshot.

A dog is also a financial commitment and not just its initial cost which can be considerable for a pedigree animal. Good quality food has to be provided and regular visits to the veterinarian for inoculations etc will be necessary from time to time. All this costs money. Also a dog needs regular grooming especially if it is a long-haired breed. This is usually a process the dog enjoys enormously and it can be fun for both owner and animal. Some dogs enjoy baths but plenty don't: how often a dog is bathed depends on its lifestyle—a showdog is constantly cleaned, a family pet does not need the same attention.

However, once you have decided that you can give a dog a good home the problem becomes which one to get. The choice is truly vast but many people already have a favorite breed, however again the same questions need to be asked, and hand on heart, honestly answered. You will be sharing your home with the dog and it does not take an expert to realize that a large dog needs a lot more space than a small one. You need to be aware of how much outside space the animal will have to move around, and how securely is it fenced—any holes and the dog will be off roaming and could prove difficult to get back. Also, an animal like a Border Collie needs enormous amounts of exercise and stimulation, so city apartment life would not work. A much smaller, less demanding type of dog such as a West Highland Terrier would be much better. Some breeds are not good with children so if small children are in the family, the more aggressive breeds like Dobermans are better

INTRODUCTION

avoided.

Different breeds have different reputations and they are not always accurate and sometimes can be completely unfair. This is where it helps to do as much research as possible about the breed, get to know its characteristics and problems, if any. Try to meet the puppy's mother (the dam)—if she is a good natured animal then the chances are that her offspring will be as well. Dogs respond very directly to the way they are treated and provided this is done with love and affection their nature will reflect this. If you know you want and can give a good home to a dog but are still unsure about which breed to opt for try to visit a dog show: chances are when you see the real thing wagging its tail in front of you it will be easy to decide on the breed. This will also provide the opportunity to ask the different breeders about the characteristics of their particular dogs—but remember they will be talking about their favorite breed and take that into consideration!

One word of warning: there are places colloquially called "puppy farms," that churn out puppies with little regard to securing good bloodlines or even healthy parents. These so-called breeders are just in it for a quick buck and are not interested in the long-term welfare of the animal. They don't of course advertise themselves as such and often attempt to hide the origins of their animals: this is one reason to visit a puppy at home with its mother and litter around it so that you can see for yourself its upbringing conditions. If a breeder refuses to let you see the puppy in its first home look for another breeder—don't be tempted by their cheaper puppies, they will almost certainly cost you more in vet's fees and heartbreak in the long run.

Once a breed is decided on, the question becomes where to get the puppy. The easiest way to find a breeder is to look on the net or get hold of one of the many specialist canine magazines where breeders advertise puppies for sale, and be prepared to pay a healthy sum for a good dog. If possible ask around about the breeder to find out in what kind of environment the animals have been reared and what sort of reputation the breeder has. Narrow down the list of possible puppies and go and have a look for yourself. This should make your mind up for you but try not to fall in love with all of them. Be practical, if you only have room for one dog only get one dog.

Another point to be aware of is that deciding to get a particular breed does not mean that you can just go out and get one—the best breeders often have waiting lists and do not breed their animals too often. Rare breeds can be especially hard to obtain. Try to be patient if you can't get what you want immediately: your forbearance will be rewarded when you get the dog you really want—a little wait is well worth the patience. Be prepared for a lot of paperwork when you get your dog, there will be all sorts of agreements and forms to sign. Consider whether to join the breed group or register with the American Kennel Club, and whether you want to join an insurance plan which will provide things such as coverage of vet fees. None of this is compulsory and only really necessary if you want to show or breed your dog, at which point this becomes a career decision.

Puppies are usually weaned and ready to leave their litter between eight and twelve weeks. A good breeder will already have had the animal checked and vaccinated before allowing it to leave for its new home; similarly along with the animal's pedigree and certificates the breeder should give you written information as to when the dog requires its next set of inoculations so that it can safely enter the outside world without the risk of catching anything.

For everyone's sake a dog must be trained to obey commands. A disobedient dog is a liability in so many ways, not only as a danger to itself but also to people. Puppy training classes are the best way to do this as the teachers are experts in how to communicate and control dogs. A well-trained dog is also important for good neighborly relations. Another essential for good relations all round is being meticulous about cleaning up after your dog, sidewalks and parks are far too often ruined by dog mess and almost nothing alienates non dog owners more than unwelcome piles of dog mess. So always carry a couple of disposable bags to collect your dog's mess—many authorities provide special bins for their disposal and a number also impose hefty fines on people who do not clean up after their dog.

Owning a dog is in many ways similar to living with a toddler, they both rely on you for their health and safety and they absolutely require as much love and attention as possible. A puppy needs plenty of clean, fresh drinking water and regular meals of nutritious food; as in later life, do not be tempted to spoil the animal with candy and chocolate, it is very bad for dogs and does their waistline and teeth no favors.

Like a small child, a puppy needs rules: it needs to know where to sleep, so provide a comfortable bed in an out of the way but still part of the family, corner. Try to provide meals at set times and in the same place and start the rudiments of training, so the dog understands basic commands such as "sit" and "no." Proper training can start later but the basics can begin immediately. The puppy has to learn quickly who is in charge (you—not him); dogs are pack animals and inherently respect the dominant dog (that's you again). House training needs to start immediately, a few puddles are only to be expected and will stop very quickly as the puppy learns to go outside.

Naming your dog should not be done on a whim: name in haste, regret later in the park when everyone turns around to see who has a dog with such a silly name. Pedigree dogs come with a long nomenclature culled from their ancestors. Sometimes a snippet of it provides a suitable name; often not. Favorite dog names are often used again and again in families and can be a popular and easy solution. Whatever name is chosen the dog needs to learn it and come to call, until then you have no hope of controlling the animal.

Puppies are notorious for chewing everything that gets within reach and your home needs to be made puppy proof in much the same way as it does with a toddler. Temporarily remove fragile, vulnerable ornaments, and tempting electric cables. Try not to leave shoes lying around: puppy owners always have exasperated tales to tell of chewed slippers and ruined chair legs. Get your dog some special puppy chews to minimize the possibility of ruined clothes or furniture. Additionally, remove any poisonous houseplants that might tempt the puppy to chew—some of them can even be fatal. It is very difficult to do this outdoors because virtually every other plant is poisonous. As a precaution stop the puppy chewing any plant except grass which they do habitually if they are feeling a little ill: grass somehow promotes vomiting and can usefully clear an obstruction or empty the stomach of something nasty.

With the best will in the world, dogs can be messy animals. Those that are free to roam the yard and house will always bring back mud or dust on their paws and often leaves and burrs in their coat as well. Additionally most breeds shed their winter coat in great tumbleweeds of hair. The bigger and shaggier the dog the more the mess. It's all part of the fun of owning a dog: if this is a step too far, then a dog is not the right companion for you: get a goldfish. Of course regular grooming, daily even during the spring coat-loss season, diminishes the amount of hair deposited around the house. Most dogs adore being groomed; the longer haired breeds require regular grooming anyway. The occasional bath is also necessary, particularly if the dog has rolled in anything smelly (a popular pastime) or gotten particularly muddy, also great fun. Special dog shampoos will help to restore a healthy shining coat. Of course with dogs such as Labrador Retrievers and Spaniels it is near impossible to keep the dog out of water, even the smallest puddle has to be jumped in, it is part of the charm of those breeds.

Dogs need regular exercise, and depending on the breed, can require a lot. Get a well fitting collar, one that's not so loose as to slip over the dog's head but not so tight that it chokes—and remember to check the fit as the animal grows. It's also a good idea to get a metal name tag with the dog's name on the front and your phone number etched on the back. That way if by chance the dogs lets lost you can be quickly contacted.

Some dogs pine when they are left, even for a short period: sometimes it can help if the radio or TV are left on because the noise provides some comfort. If your dog has to be left alone for much of the time consider getting him another dog for company, they might get up to mischief but they are unlikely to get bored. As a pack animal dogs enjoy the company of other dogs, although it may take a while for an older dog to accept and adjust a younger incomer. It's amazing just how jealous some dogs can get, but they usually get over it after a few weeks.

Sometimes a dog has to be left behind while the family has to go away, in which case if he can't stay with a reliable friend you need to find a kennel with a good reputation. The best way to do this is to ask around, people are usually very quick to say which are the good and bad places their pets loved or hated. When boarding them in a kennel leave an unwashed jumper or T-shirt or anything that smells of you, to provide a bit of home security and tell your dog you love him and that you'll be home soon. He won't understand, of course, but you will both feel a bit better for it.

COLLIE

Collie refers to various breeds of herding dog originating primarily in Scotland. The fictional Lassie, star of movies, books, and television shows, was a rough collie, which helped to popularize Collies in the United States and the United Kingdom, as well as in many other countries. The Collie Club of America is one of the oldest breed-specific clubs in existence in the United States (founded in 1886). The farm collie was a generic term for a wide range of herding dogs common in North America until the middle of the 20th century. Shetland Sheepdogs (commonly known as "Shelties") are sometimes mistakenly called Miniature Collies, but they are a completely different breed of distinct origin. Collies come in two varieties of the breed based on coat length in America; in the UK these are shown as separate breeds. The rough collie is the collie seen in films and on television (e.g., Lassie). The downy undercoat is covered by a long, dense, coarse outer coat with a notable ruff around the neck, feathers about the legs, a petticoat on the abdomen, and a frill on the hindquarters. The smooth collie likewise has a double coat, but the outer one is short and dense, albeit there is a notable ruff around the neck. Both rough and smooth varieties are available in four distinct colors. Sable collies are generally the most recognizable, the choice of the Lassie television and movie producers. The sable color on these dogs can range from a light blonde color to a deep reddish-brown, with any hue in between possible. Tri-colour dogs are mostly black and white with tan markings. Blue Merle collies are best described as tri-colour dogs whose black has been diluted to a mottled gray-blue color. Collies typically live an average of 12 to 14 years. Collies are known to be generally sweet and protective. They are generally easy to train due to a high level of intelligence and a willingness to please. Some collies are a bit clingy, but this is often seen as an overdeveloped sense of loyalty.

GERMAN SHEPHERD

The German Shepherd Dog is a large and strong dog. The fur is a double-coat and can be either short or long haired. Although the black and tan saddle may be most recognizable, German Shepherds come in a variety of colors and patterns though not all are accepted by the various breed clubs or FCI. The German lines of the German Shepherd tend to be larger dogs with a broader head and darker coat. With the "Americanization" of the German Shepherd, many of the dogs have become smaller with less sloping to their hips. These lines can also show more of the silver and black coat coloring as opposed to the black and tan/brown coat of the German lines.

Well-bred GSDs have powerful jaws and strong teeth, can develop a strong sense of loyalty and obedience, and can be trained to attack and release on command. Poorly bred GSDs such as those from puppy mills can be fearful, overly aggressive, or both. GSDs, along with Pit Bulls, Rottweilers, and Dobermans, are often perceived as inherently dangerous, and are the target of Breed Specific Legislation in several countries. GSDs are often used as guard, seeing eye, and police dogs and more specifically search and rescue, narcotics dogs, and bomb scenting dogs which further contributes to the perception of their being a dangerous breed. However, many GSDs function perfectly well as search dogs and family pets - roles where aggressive behavior is unsuitable.

GSDs' sense of loyalty and emotional bond with their owners is almost impossible to describe. They have a keen intuition or bond which is highly in tune with their owner/handler. Separation trauma is one reason they are now used less often in guide dog roles, since guide dogs are typically trained from puppyhood by one owner/handler prior to final placement with their employer, i.e, new owner.

OLD ENGLISH SHEEPDOG

The Old English Sheepdog is a breed of dog used for herding livestock, and as a pet. They are best known for their shaggy grey and white fur which also covers their face, including their eyes, which leads some casual observers to wonder how they can see. With very few exceptions, the OES's tail is cut off at or below the first joint as puppies. The procedure, known as docking or "bobbing" the tail produces the panda-like rear end. Puppies are born with jet black and white fur further likening them to the panda bear. It is only after the puppy coat has been shed that the more common gray or silver shaggy hair appears. Males generally weigh 70 to 100 pounds(45 kg); females, 60 to 80 pounds. They stand around 22 inches at the withers. Their long coats can be any shade of gray, grizzle, blue, or blue merle, with optional white markings. The undercoat is water resistant. The Old English Sheepdog's abundant coat is an effective insulator in both hot and cold weather. This breed is intelligent, funny, social, and adaptable, although they sometimes seem to not be all that intelligent on first impressions. It generally gets along well with children, other dogs, other pets, and visitors. Like all herding breeds, it requires plenty of exercise, both mental and physical. They are bubbly and playful, and some times may be stubborn, depending on their mood. Sheepdogs are excellent, intuitive and loving companions, even earning the title "babysitter" or "Dear Nanny" around young children. The herding instinct that has been carried down through the generations is still astonishing. The long coat requires thorough brushing at least weekly, preferably from the base of the hairs to keep the thick undercoat hair mat and tangle free. Brushing only over the top of the longer outside (guard) hairs can compact the undercoat and promote mats.

AFGHAN HOUND

The Afghan Hound is a very old sighthound dog breed. Distinguished by its thick, fine, silky coat and its tail with a ring curl at the end, the breed acquired its unique features in the cold mountains of Afghanistan, where it was originally used to hunt wolves, foxes, and gazelles. The Afghan Hound is tall, standing 24 to 29 inches (63-74 cm) in height and weighing 45 to 60 pounds (20-30 kg). The coat may be any colour, but white markings, particularly on the head, are discouraged; many individuals have a black facial mask. Some are almost white, but particolor hounds (white with islands of red or black) are not acceptable and may indicate impure breeding. The long, fine-textured coat requires considerable care and grooming. The long topknot and the shorter-haired saddle on the back in the mature dog are distinctive features of the Afghan Hound coat. The high hipbones and unique small ring on the end of the tail are also characteristics of the breed. The temperament of the typical Afghan Hound can be aloof and dignified, but happy and clownish when playing. Afghans hounds are a relatively healthy breed; major health issues are allergies, and cancer. Sensitivity to anesthesia is an issue the Afghan hound shares with the rest of the sighthound group, as sighthounds have relatively low levels of body fat. Afghan hounds as a whole are a fairly long-lived breed, often living 13-14 years. The breed was always thought to date back at least to the pre-Christian era, and recent discoveries by researchers studying ancient DNA have revealed that the Afghan Hound is in fact one of the most ancient dog breeds, dating back for many thousands of years. Its original native name, Tazi, betrays its connection to the very similar Tasy breed of Russia.

BASSET HOUND

The Basset Hound is a scent hound, bred to hunt by scent. Their sense of smell for tracking is second only to that of the Bloodhound. The name Basset derives from the French word "bas" meaning "low;" "basset" meaning, literally, "rather low." These dogs are around 33 to 38 cm (13 to 15 inches) in height at the withers. They usually weigh between 50-70lbs. They have smooth, short-haired coats but a rough haired hound is possible. Although any hound color is considered acceptable by breed standards, Bassets are generally tricolor (black, tan, and white), open red and white (red spots on white fur), closed red and white (a solid red color with white feet and tails), and lemon and white. Their tails are long and tapering and stand upright with a curve. The tail should also be tipped in white. This is so they are easily seen when hunting/tracking through large brush or weeds. The breed is also known for its hanging skin structure, which causes the face to have a permanently sad look; this, for many people, adds to the breed's charm. The dewlap, seen as the loose, elastic skin around the neck and the trailing ears help trap the scent of what they are tracking. Like other hounds, Basset Hounds are often difficult to obedience train. Many will obey commands when offered a food reward, but will "forget" the training when a reward is not present. They are notoriously difficult to housebreak. The breed has a strong hunting instinct and will give chase or follow a scent if given the opportunity. They should be trained in recall; failing that, they should be kept on a leash when out on walks.

BEAGLE

Beagles are scent hounds used primarily for tracking deer, bear, and other game. Beagle-type dogs have existed for over 5 centuries, but the breed as popularly known was developed in the United Kingdom about 150 years ago. The Beagle has a smooth, somewhat oval skull; a medium length, square-cut muzzle; a black, gumdrop nose, large, hound-like hazel or brown eyes; long, velveteen, low-set ears (big), turning towards the cheeks slightly and rounded at the tips; a medium-length, strong neck without folds in the skin; a broad chest narrowing to a tapered abdomen and waist; a short, slightly curved tail; an overall muscular body; and a medium-length, smooth, hard coat. The Beagle's droopy ears should be very soft on the outside and fabricy on the inside. One standard calls for ideally shaped beagles to be twice as long as tall, and twice as tall as wide. They appear in a range of colors, not limited to the familiar tricolor (white with large black areas and light brown spots). Some tricolored dogs have a color pattern referred to as "broken." These dogs have mostly white coats with slightly circular patches of black and brown hair. Two-color varieties are always white with colored areas, including such colors as "lemon", a very light tan; "red", a reddish, almost orangish brown; and "liver", a darker brown (liver is the only colour not allowed in the British Standard). The American Kennel Club and the Canadian Kennel Club recognize two separate varieties of Beagle: the 13-inch for hounds less than 13 inches (330 mm), and the 15-inch for those between 13 and 15 inches (330 and 380 mm). The Kennel Club (UK) and FCI affiliated clubs recognize a single type, with a height of between 13 and 16 inches (330 and 400 mm). These standard dogs can reach 35 lb (16 kg) or more.

BORZOI

Borzoi can come in any color or color combination. As a general approximation, "long haired greyhound" is a useful description. The long top-coat is silky and quite flat, with varying degrees of waviness or curling. The soft undercoat thickens in winter or cold climates but is shed in hot weather to prevent overheating. In its texture and distribution over the body, the Borzoi coat is unique.

The Borzoi is a large variety of sighthound, with males frequently reaching in excess of 100 pounds (45 kg). Males should stand at least 28 inches (about 70 centimeters) at the shoulder, while females shouldn't be less than 26 inches (about 66 centimeters). The Borzoi is a quiet, intelligent, moderately active, independent dog. They adapt very well to suburban living, provided they have a spacious yard and regular opportunities for free exercise.

Most adult Borzoi are almost mute, barking only very rarely. They are gentle, sensitive dogs with gracious house-manners and a natural respect for humans. Many Borzoi do well in competitive obedience and agility trials with the right kind of training, but it is not an activity that comes naturally to them. They are fast learners who quickly become bored with repetitive, apparently pointless, activity, and they can be very stubborn when they are not properly motivated. These are dogs used to pursue, or "course," game and they have a strong instinct to chase things that run from them. Borzoi are built for speed and can cover incredible distances in a very short time. They need a fully-fenced yard if automobile traffic is present within several miles of their home. For off-lead exercise they need a very large field or park, either fully fenced or well away from any traffic, to ensure their safety.

DACHSHUND

The dachshund is a short-legged, elongated dog breed of the hound family. The breed's name is German and literally means "badger dog," from Dachs "badger" and Hund "dog". Due to the long, narrow build, they are sometimes referred to in the United States and elsewhere as a wiener dog, hot dog, or sausage dog. According to kennel club standards, the miniature variety differs from the full-size only by size and weight, however, offspring from miniature parents must never weigh more than the miniature standard to be considered a miniature as well. A full-grown standard dachshund averages 16 to 28 pounds. (7 to 12.7 kg), while the miniature variety typically weighs less than 11 lb. (5 kg). As early as the 1990s, owners' use of a third weight class became common, the "tweenie," which included those dachshunds that fell in between standard and miniature, ranging from 10 to 15 lb. (4.5 to 6.75 kg). Dachshunds come in three coat varieties. The most common and associated with the dachshund is the smooth coated dog. The next most recognised is the long coat. The wire haired dachshund is least common. Many people cannot even recognize it as being a Dachshund. Wire Dachshund owners often hear people saying that their dog is a schnauzer or even a yorkie, which is just not the case. Dachshunds are playful, fun dogs, known for their propensity to chase small animals, birds and tennis balls with great determination and ferocity. Many dachshunds are strong-headed or stubborn, making them a challenge to train. Dachshunds are known for their devotion and loyalty to their owners. If left alone many doxies will whine until they have companionship. The dachshund's temperament may vary greatly from dog to dog. Although the dachshund is generally an energetic dog, some are laid back. Due to this dog's behavior, it is not the dog for everyone. A bored Dachshund will become destructive.

RHODESIAN RIDGEBACK

The Rhodesian Ridgeback is a breed from Southern Africa. They originated in Rhodesia (modern day Zimbabwe). Some Ridgebacks are born without ridges, and until recently, most ridgeless puppies were culled, or euthanized, at birth. Today, many breeders opt instead to spay and neuter these offspring to ensure they will not be bred. Dogs should be 25-27 inches (63-69 cm) at the withers and weigh approximately 85 lb (36.5 kg FCI Standard), however some have been known to reach up to 160 lb, Bitches 24-26 inches (61-66 cm) and approximately 70 lb (32 kg). Ridgebacks are typically muscular and have a light wheaten to red wheaten coat which should be short and dense, sleek and glossy in appearance but neither woolly nor silky. Ridgebacks have a strong, smooth tail, which is usually carried in a gentle curve upwards. The eyes should be round and should reflect the dog's color (pigment, not coat color) -- dark eyes with a black nose (regardless of coat color), amber eyes with a liver nose. The liver nose is a recessive gene so therefore is not as common as a black nose; some breeders believe the inclusion of livernoses in a breeding program is necessary for maintaining the vibrancy of the coat. Despite their athletic, sometimes imposing exterior, the Ridgeback has a sensitive side. Excessively harsh training methods that might be tolerated by a sporting or working dog will likely backfire on a Ridgeback. Intelligent to a fault, the Ridgeback accepts correction as long as it is fair and justified, and as long as it comes from someone he knows and trusts. Francis R. Barnes, who wrote the first standard in 1922, acknowledged that "rough treatment ... should never be administered to these dogs, especially when they are young. They go to pieces with handling of that kind."

BICHON FRISE

The Bichon Frisé descended from the Barbet or Water Spaniel, from which came the name "Barbichon", later shortened to "Bichon". The Bichons were divided into four categories: the Bichon Maltais, the Bichon Bolognais, the Bichon Havanais and the Bichon Tenerife. All originated in the Mediterranean area. Because of their merry disposition, they traveled much and were often used as items of barter by sailors as they moved from continent to continent. The dogs found early success in Spain and it is generally felt that Spanish seamen introduced the breed to the Canary Island of Tenerife. In the 1300s, Italian sailors rediscovered the little dogs on their voyages and are credited with returning them to the continent, where they became great favorites of Italian nobility. Often, as was the style of the day with dogs in the courts, they were cut "lion style." The Bichon Frise has a mild attitude but can be over excited. The well-bred Bichon Frisé is gentle-mannered, sensitive, playful, and affectionate. A cheerful attitude is a prominent hallmark. Most Bichons enjoy socializing with people and other dogs, and are best when there is a lot of activity around them. They are a non-moulting breed and are suitable for people with allergies. Care must be taken to keep the face of a Bichon Frisé clean and trimmed, as eye discharge and mucus tend to accumulate in the hair that grows in front of their eyes, which can lead to serious problems. Their hair should be brushed daily, but if not possible, at least 2-3 times a week. The hair will puff up if groomed correctly, and their tails curl over their back. This breed is prone to knots in the hair. It is important to remove hair tangles prior to shampooing, lest more tangles develop, causing mats. The Bichon lives around about 13-16 yrs, but has been known to live to 21.

BULLDOG

The bulldog is a relatively small but stocky breed, with a compact body and short, sturdy limbs. Its shape results in a waddle-like gait. Bulldogs are known for their short muzzles and the saggy skin on their faces, creating the apparent "frown" that has become a trademark of the breed. Bulldogs come in a variety of colors and ideally have a smooth, short coat. The size for a mature male is about 50 pounds (25 kg); that for mature females is about 40 pounds (23.7 kg). The temperament of the English Bulldog is generally docile, friendly and gregarious, but are known to be fiercely loyal and defensive and, because of their strength, could make good guard dogs. However most breeders have worked to breed aggression out of the breed. The bulldog is prone to some health problems, such as hip dysplasia and breathing problems. Due to their generally low energy levels, and their quiet nature (they rarely bark without cause) they make great apartment pets as well as household pets. If not properly neutered and spayed adult animals may develop aggressive tendencies.

Bulldogs require daily cleaning of their face folds to avoid unwanted infections caused by moisture accumulation. Daily teeth brushing with a regular human soft toothbrush using a vet approved toothpaste is also recommended.

The term "bulldog" was first used around 1568 and might have been applied to various ancestors of modern bulldog breeds. Unfortunately, this group never picked a specific breed standard, and in 1891 the two top bulldogs, bitch Orry and Dockleaf, were greatly different in appearance. King Orry was reminiscent of the original bulldogs—lighter boned and very athletic. Dockleaf was smaller and heavier set—more like modern bulldogs. Dockleaf was declared the winner that year.

DALMATIAN

The Dalmatian is most noted for its white coat with either black or liver spots. Although other color variations do exist, any color markings other than black or liver are a disqualification in purebred Dalmatians. The famous spotted coat is unique to the Dalmatian breed; no other purebred dog breed sports the flashy spotted markings. The breed takes its name from the Croatian province of Dalmatia, where it is believed to have originated. This popular breed is a well-muscled, midsized dog with superior endurance. Known for its elegance, the Dalmatian has a body type similar to the Pointer, to which it may be related. The feet are round and compact with well-arched toes. The ears are thin, tapering toward the tip, set fairly high and carried close to the head. The ideal Dalmatian should stand between 19 and 24 inches at the withers and weight from 45 to 70 pounds fully grown. Breed standards for showing for more specific sizes; the UK standard for instance, calls for a height between 22 and 24 inches. Males are generally slightly larger than females. Puppies are born with completely white fur, though the beginning of spots can sometimes be seen under the skin of a newborn pup. Any areas of color at birth are a "patch", and patches are a disqualifying fault in the breed standard. Spots will become evident after a week or so, and develop rapidly during the first few weeks. Spots will continue to develop both in number and size throughout the dog's life, though at a slower pace as the dog gets older. Given freedom to roam, they will take multi-day trips on their own across the countryside. In today's urban environment, they will not likely survive such excursions and must be contained. Their energetic and playful nature make them good companions for children and they have an instinctive fondness for humans and horses. These qualities make them somewhat "unbreakable", and forgiving of rough handling by children.

POINTER (GERMAN SHORTHAIRED)

The German Shorthaired Pointer is a breed developed in the 1800s in Germany for hunting. This gun dog was developed by crossing the old Spanish pointer with a number of other breeds and breed types including scent hounds, tracking hounds, French Braques, and English Pointer to create a lean, athletic, and responsive all around hunting dog. Some authorities consider it to be the most versatile of all gun dogs and its intelligence and affectionate nature make it a popular companion dog for active owners. The breed is lean, athletic, and graceful yet powerful with strong hindquarters that make it able to move rapidly and turn quickly. It has moderately long flop ears set high on the head. Its muzzle is long, broad, and strong, allowing it to retrieve even heavy furred game. Its profile should be straight or slightly Roman-nosed; any dished appearance to the profile (such as seen in the Pointer) is incorrect. Their eyes are generally light hazel in colour. Its tail is commonly docked, although this is now prohibited in some countries. The German Shorthaired Pointer's coat is short and flat. It should have a dense underful protected by stiff guard hairs that makes the coat water resistant and better suited to cold weather than that of the English Pointer for example. The color can be a dark brown, correctly referred to in English as liver (incorrectly called chocolate or chestnut), black (although any area of black is cause for disqualification in American Kennel Club and Canadian Kennel Club sanctioned shows), or either color with white. Commonly the head is a solid or nearly solid color and the body is speckled or ticked with liver, white or black, with saddles or large patches of solid color. Various breed standards set its height at the withers anywhere between 21 and 25 inches, making this a medium breed. Adults typically weigh from 45 to 70 lbs (24 to 32 kg), with the female being usually slightly shorter and lighter than the male.

RETRIEVER (GOLDEN)

The Golden Retriever is a popular breed of dog, originally developed to retrieve downed fowl during hunting. It is one of the most common family dogs as it is easy to handle, very tolerant, and normally very happy and friendly. It is a low-maintenance dog and thrives on attention, regular exercise, a balanced diet, and regular veterinary check-ups. Golden Retrievers are particularly valued for their high level of sociability towards people and willingness to learn. Because of this, they are commonly used as Guide dogs and Search and Rescue dogs. The Golden is athletic, well balanced, and symmetrical. This large breed is similar in appearance to the yellow Labrador Retriever, especially when young. The most obvious difference is the Golden Retriever's luxurious coat, which varies in shades of goldish yellow.

Today's Golden Retrievers fall into two groups: English and American. These two types are merely variations of the Golden Retriever breed as a whole, and differ only in aesthetics. English Goldens are easily recognized by their longer, light cream-colored coats, which sometimes appear white. This type is bigger-boned, shorter, with a more square head and/or muzzle. They are more common in Europe, so breeders of this type in America may import their dogs to improve bloodlines. A Golden Retriever of English breeding can have a coat color in the color range of all shades of gold or cream, but not including red nor mahogany. A few white hairs on the chest are acceptable.

The coat is dense and waterproof, and may be straight or moderately wavy. It usually lies flat against the belly. The American Kennel Club (AKC) standard states that the coat is a "rich, lustrous golden of various shades", disallowing coats that are extremely light or extremely dark.

RETRIEVER (LABRADOR)

The Labrador Retriever, is one of several kinds of retriever, and is the most popular breed of dog (by registered ownership) in both the United States and the United Kingdom. The breed is exceptionally friendly, intelligent, energetic and good natured, making them excellent companions and working dogs. Labrador Retrievers respond well to praise and positive attention. They are also well known as enjoying water, since historically, they were selectively bred for retrieving in water environments as "gun dogs" and as companions in waterfowl hunting. Many fishermen originally used the Lab to assist in bringing nets to shore; the dog would grab the floating corks on the ends of the nets and pull them to shore. They were brought to the Poole area of England, then the hub of the Newfoundland fishing trade, and became prized amongst the gentry as sporting dogs. Labradors are relatively large with males typically weighing 27 to 36 kg (60 to 80 lb) and females 23 to 32 kg (45 to 70 lb). Their coats are short and smooth, and they possess a straight, powerful tail like that of an otter. The majority of the characteristics of this breed with the exception of colour are the result of breeding to produce a working retriever.

As with some other breeds, the English (typically "show") and the American (typically "working" or "field") lines differ. Labs are bred in England as a medium size dog, shorter and stockier with fuller faces and a slightly calmer nature than their American counterparts which are bred as a larger lighter-built dog. No distinction is made by the American Kennel Club (AKC), but the two classifications come from different breeding. The otter-like tail and webbed toes of the Labrador Retriever make them excellent swimmers.

SETTER (IRISH)

The Irish Setter, also known as the Red Setter, is a breed of gundog and family dog. The term Irish Setter is commonly used to encompass the Show-bred dog recognized by the AKC as well as the field-bred Red Setter recognized by the Field Dog Stud Book. The coat is moderately long and silky and of a deep red color. It requires frequent brushing to maintain its condition and keep it mat-free. The undercoat is abundant in winter weather. Irish Setters range in height from 25 to 27 inches (64-69 cm), males weigh 60 to 70 pounds (27-32 kg) and females 53 to 64 pounds (24-29 kg). The FCI Breed Standard for the Irish Setter stipulates males: 23 to 26.5 inches (58-67 cm), females: 21.5 to 24.5 inches (55-62 cm). In general, Irish Setters are friendly, enjoy human company, and actively look for other dogs with which to play. They are affectionate and like to be petted. Irish Setters are excellent with children. Due to the breed's need for frequent activity, this is an inappropriate dog for inactive families or apartment dwellers. Irish Setters are not aggressive, although can bark to protect the area from strangers. They have been marked as being stupid, but are really quite intelligent. The breed Irish Red Setter was developed in Ireland in the 1700s from the Old Spanish Pointer, setting spaniels, and early Scottish setters. Early Irish Setters were white with red blotches on their coats, but today the Setter's coat is a rich mahogany color. The Irish Red and White Setter is more closely related to those early Setters. The Irish Setter's name in Gaelic is Madra rua or "red dog". Originally, the Irish Setter was bred for hunting, specifically for setting or pointing upland gamebirds. They are similar to other members of the setter family such as the English Setter and Gordon Setter. Irish Setters are extremely swift, with an excellent sense of smell and are hardy over any terrain and in any climate. The Irish Setter is used for all types of hunting. It even works well on wetlands.

SPANIEL (COCKER)

The American Cocker Spaniel is a breed of dog that originated in the United Kingdom and was brought to Canada and the United States in the late 1800s. American Cocker Spaniels were given their own AKC Stud Book in the early 1900s. By 1946, the English Cocker Spaniel was distinct enough in type from the "American" variety, that the American Kennel Club established it as a breed separate from the American Cocker Spaniel. It was given its own Stud Book and that left the "American" type to be known as the Cocker Spaniel in the United States. They are in the sporting breed group of dogs and are the smallest of their group. American Cocker Spaniels were used to flush out birds and prey from the brush so their masters could shoot it. The signature trait of the American Cocker Spaniel is its dark, expressive eyes that reflect a happy, loving, and active nature. Cockers are a dropped eared breed (pendulous ears) and the mature Cocker is shown in a full feathered, silky coat. After its show career ends, the fur is often trimmed into a "puppy cut," shortened on the legs, sides and belly, that is easier to keep whether as a pet, performance dog, or hunting companion. Cockers weigh an average of 18 to 28 pounds. The ideal height of an adult female at the withers is 14 inches; the ideal height for males is 15 inches. An adult male who is over 15.5 inches, or an adult female over 14.5 inches would be disqualified in a conformation show. Bone and head size should be in proportion to the overall balance of the dog.

Their temperament is typically joyful and trusting. The ideal Cocker temperament is merry, outgoing, and eager to please everyone. They can be good with children and usually sociable and gentle with other pets. They tend to be "softer" dogs who do not do well with rough or harsh training.

VIZSLA

The Hungarian Vizsla, pronounced VEEZH-la (zh as in vision), is a dog breed that originated in Hungary. Vizslas are known as excellent hunting dogs, and also have a level personality making them suited for families. The Hungarian Wirehaired Vizsla was created by cross-breeding the Hungarian Shorthaired Vizsla with the German Wirehaired Pointer during the 1930s. The Vizsla, as described in the AKC standard, is a medium-sized short-coated hunting dog of distinguished appearance and bearing. Robust but rather lightly built; the coat is an attractive golden rust color. The coat could also be described as a copper/brown color. They are lean dogs, and have defined muscles, and a coat a lot like a weimaraner, a silver colored dog. Small areas of white on the fore-chest and on the toes are permissible but undesirable. The tail is normally docked to two-thirds of the original length. The ideal male is 22 inches(0.55 m) to 24 inches (0.61 m). The ideal female is 21inches (0.53 m) to 23 inches (0.58 m). Commonly weighing 40-65 lbs (18.14-29.48 kg). Because the Vizsla is meant to be a medium-sized hunter, any dog measuring more than 1½ inches (3.8 cm) over or under these limits must be disqualified. Vizslas are lively, gentle-mannered, loyal, caring and highly affectionate. They quickly form close bonds with their owners, including children. Often they are referred to as "velcro" dogs because of their loyalty and affection. They are quiet dogs, only barking if necessary or provoked. They are natural hunters with an excellent ability to take training. Not only are they great pointers, but they are excellent retrievers as well. They will retrieve on land and in the water, making the most of their natural instincts. Vizslas are excellent swimmers and often swim in pools if one is available. Like all gun dogs, Vizslas require a good deal of exercise to remain healthy and happy. Vizslas are one of only seven breeds recognised as having all three HPR (Hunt, Point, Retreive) skills.

WEIMARANER

The Weimaraner is a silver-grey breed developed originally for hunting. Rather than having a specific purpose such as pointing or flushing, the Weimaraner is an all purpose dog. The Weimaraner is loyal and loving to his family, an incredible hunter, and a fearless guardian of his family and territory. The name comes from the Grand Duke of Weimar, Charles August, whose court enjoyed hunting. The Weimaraner is elegant, noble, and athletic in appearance. The tails, which may be amber or gray, are kept short. In some cases, tails are docked and dewclaws are removed, the tail usually docked at birth to a third of its natural length. This breed's short, smooth gray coat and its unusual eyes give it a regal appearance different from any other breed. The eyes may be light amber, gray, or blue-gray. The coat may range from mouse-gray (grayish beige or tan) to silver-gray. The nose should be a dark gray. Where the fur is thin or non-existent, inside the ears or on the lips, for example, the skin should be a pinkish "flesh" tone rather than white or black. According to the AKC standard, the male Weimaraner stands between 25 and 27 inches (63-68 cm) at the withers. Females are between 23 and 25 inches (58-63 cm). Of course, there are many dogs taller or shorter than the breed standard. The breed is not heavy for its height, and males normally weigh roughly 70-85 pounds. Females are generally between 55-70 lbs. A Weimaraner carries its weight proudly and gives the appearance of a muscular, athletic dog. Weimaraners are fast and powerful dogs, but are also suitable home animals given appropriate training. These dogs are not as sociable towards strangers like other hunting dogs such as the Labrador and Golden Retrievers. Weimaraners are very protective of their family and are very territorial. They are aloof to strangers, and must be thoroughly socialized when young to prevent aggression.

AIREDALE TERRIER

The Airedale Terrier (often shortened to "Airedale") is a terrier dog breed originating from Airedale in Yorkshire, England. It is sometimes called the "King of Terriers" because it is the largest of the terrier breeds, 50 to 70 pounds (23-32 kg). The breed has also been called the Waterside Terrier, because it was bred originally to hunt otters. Like many terriers, the breed has a 'broken' coat: a harsh, wiry topcoat with a soft, fur-like undercoat. Because of this coat, Airedales do not significantly shed.

The correct coat color is a black saddle, with a tan head, ears and legs; or a dark grizzle saddle (black mixed with gray and white). Both are acceptable in the AKC breed standard. Airedales have a normal 'scissors bite', where the top teeth close over the bottom. Airedales' teeth are the largest among terriers. They can be used as a working dog and also as a hunter and retriever. In 1886, the Kennel Club of England formally recognised the Airedale Terrier breed. Well-to-do hunters of the era were typically accompanied by pack of hounds and several terriers, often running them both together. The hounds would scent and pursue the quarry and the terriers would "go to ground" or enter into the quarry's burrow and make the kill. Terriers were often the sporting dog of choice for the common man. Early sporting terriers needed to be big enough to tackle the quarry, but not so big as to prevent them from maneuvering through the quarry's underground lair. The Airedale was extensively used in World War I to carry messages to soldiers behind enemy lines and transport mail. They were also used by the Red Cross to find wounded soldiers on the battlefield. There are numerous tales of Airedales delivering their messages despite terrible injury. Before the adoption of the German Shepherd as the dog of choice for law enforcement and search and rescue work, the Airedale terrier often filled this role.

AMERICAN STAFFORDSHIRE TERRIER

The American Staffordshire Terrier is descended from American dog fighting breeds and was intended to be a show strain of the American Pit Bull Terrier. American Staffordshire Terriers were first recognized by the American Kennel Club in 1936. They are a member of the Terrier and Molosser groups. The American Staffordshire Terrier is a large dog that ranges from 16 to 19 inches (40 to 50 cm) at the withers, and weighs from 57 to 67 pounds (26 to 30 kg). The breed is long, muscular and strong, and gives the impression of great strength and agility for his size. The chest is deep and broad, and the neck is heavy. The dog has a broad skull, pronounced cheek muscles, and strong jaws. The ears may be half prick, rose, or cropped. The coat is short and glossy and can be of any color although all white, mostly white, liver, and black and tan are not encouraged. These dogs should be courageous, tenacious, friendly, extremely attentive, and extraordinarily devoted. Originally an all-around farm dog, hunter, and family companion, American Staffordshire Terriers should be highly stable around both children and other domesticated animals (such as livestock). Exceptionally friendly, well cared for American Staffordshire Terriers are not natural watchdogs, often failing to bark at the door upon the arrival of visitors. A lack of protective and/or aggressive behaviour, accompanied by fearlessness, is generally a good sign. Such a dog is stable with children, friendly with new animals, and easily cared for by pet sitters. As an added bonus, a thorough familiarity with "normal" situations - the advent of the mailman or petsitter - will make "abnormal" or dangerous situations impeccably clear to a devoted pet. Such devotion will motivate a dog of any lineage to lay down its life to protect an owner, friend, or even a stranger in need. The American Staffordshire Terrier temperament is not ideal for every owner or family.

BULL TERRIER

Bull Terriers are thick-set and muscular with a short, dense coat. Acceptable colours are white, (skin pigmentation and markings on the head are not to be penalised in the show ring in the UK), any colour other than white, or any colour with white markings (although Blue and liver highly undesirable). The bull terrier's most distinctive feature is its head, described as 'egg shaped' when viewed from the front, almost flat at the top, with a Roman muzzle sloping evenly down to the end of the nose with no stop. The unique triangular eyes are small, dark, and closely set. The body is full and round, while the shoulders are robust and muscular and the tail is carried horizontally. It walks with a jaunty gait, and is popularly known as the 'gladiator of the canine race'.

There is no set height or weight of the breed but the average is, Height: 16-22 inches (40-56 cm.), Weight: 35-80 pounds (15-36 kg.). Bull Terriers are generally friendly dogs. Their physical strength is matched by their intelligence, and both body and mind need to be kept active. They are very affectionate dogs that love human company, so it is not a good idea to leave them alone for long periods of time as with their strong jaws they can cause severe damage if bored. Bull Terriers are particularly good with children and can stand a great deal of abuse due to their high pain threshold. They are protective of children in their charge. The American Temperament Test Society, Inc. (ATTS), a not-for-profit organisation that promotes uniform temperament testing for dog breeds, gives the Bull Terrier a pass rate of 91.5%. The average for all breeds is 81.5%. While not definitive, this does suggest that the Bull Terrier has a more than usually even temperament. Their lifespan is somewhere between 10 and 14 years, although they can live longer -- the oldest bitch on record being an Australian housepet dubbed "Puppa Trout" who remained sprightly into her 17th year.

CAIRN TERRIER

The breed standard can be found on the Cairn Terrier Club of America website. The current standard was approved on May 10, 1938 and it was adopted from the The Kennel Club of Great Britain. According to the American standard, dogs should weigh 14 pounds and stand 10" at the withers. Females should weigh 13 pounds and stand 9.5" at the withers. A Cairn's appearance may vary from this standard. It is common for a Cairn to stand between 9 and 13 inches (23-33 cm) at the withers and weigh 13 to 18 pounds (6 to 8 kg). European Cairns tend to be larger than American Cairns. Due to irresponsible breeding, many Cairns available today are much smaller or much larger than the breed standard. Cairns that have had puppy mill backgrounds can weigh as little as 7 pounds or as much as 27 pounds. The Cairn Terrier has a harsh, weather-resistant outer coat that can be cream, wheaten, red, sandy, gray, or brindled in any of these colors. Pure black, black and tan, and white are not permitted by many kennel clubs. While registration of white Cairns was once permitted, after 1917 the American Kennel Club required them to be registered as West Highland White Terriers. A notable characteristic of Cairns is that brindled Cairns frequently change color throughout their lifetime. It is not uncommon for a brindled Cairn to become progressively more black or silver as it ages. The Cairn is double-coated, with a soft, dense undercoat and a harsh outer coat. A well-groomed Cairn has a rough-and-ready appearance, free of artifice or exaggeration. Cairn Terriers are intelligent, strong, and loyal. Like most terriers, they are stubborn and strong-willed, and love to dig after real or imagined prey. Cairn Terriers have a strong prey instinct and will need comprehensive training. However, they are highly intelligent and, although very willful, can be trained. Although it is often said that they are disobedient, this is not the case provided correct training is applied.

MINIATURE SCHNAUZER

Miniature Schnauzers developed from crosses between the Standard Schnauzer and one or more smaller breeds such as the Poodle, Miniature Pinscher, or Affenpinscher. They should be compact, muscular, and be "square" in build (the height at the withers should be the same as the length of the body). They have long beards, eyebrows, and feathering on the legs. In the USA, ears are sometimes cropped to stand upright and the tail is often docked short. British schnauzers have uncropped ears, as ear cropping is illegal in the United Kingdom. Their coats are wiry (when hand-stripped,) and do not shed, which adds to their appeal as house pets. Miniature Schnauzers that are shown at dog shows needs to be hand-stripped to achieve the wiry texture that the breed standard calls for. Pets that are not shown, can be clippered. This will however turn the coat soft and make the dog lose color. Height is 12 to 15 inches (30.5 to 38 cm) at the withers (American standard) or 30-35cm (FCI, German standard) at the withers, and they generally weigh 11 to 20 pounds (4.5 to 7 kg). They are also highly loyal to their owner and can be very energetic, but if not given proper exercise or a balanced diet, they will gain weight very quickly. Miniature Schnauzers are extremely vocal dogs, and are known for their barking. This is because they are excellent protectors of their home and will alert their owners to anyone that may be coming. However some dogs of the breed will bark at even the slightest noises. This amount of unnecessary barking can usually be controlled by training if the owner has patience with the dog. The Miniature Schnauzer is often guarded of strangers until the owners of the home welcome the guest, upon which they are typically very friendly to them. The breed is very good with children recognizing that they need gentle play.

PARSON RUSSELL TERRIER

The Parson Russell Terrier was the first Kennel Club recognized variant of the Jack Russell Terrier, first drawn into the UK Kennel Club in 1990, and into the American Kennel Club in 2001. The Parson Russell Terrier is a balanced, square dog, very similar in form to other Russell Terriers, but is largely a show breed rather than a working dog. Like all Jack Russells, the Parson Russell Terrier is descended from early white-bodied fox-working terriers used in the hunt field. The Kennel Club Parson Russell terriers are dogs that reside at the top end of Jack Russell height spectrum (12-14 inches) although it must be pointed out that taller Jack Russell types do exist as "Jack Russells" in working Jack Russell Terrier clubs in the United Kingdom and the United States.

The name "Parson Russell" Terrier was chosen by the American Kennel Club because of a compromise with the Jack Russell Terrier Club of America. It is likely that there will be more changes before the various Russell Terriers are definitively categorized. Parsons love routine and structure, not to be confused with constraint. Terriers in general do not like to be confined in kennels and unless kennels are constructed of "thick." welded steel, confinement will not be achieved. If leaving the Parson home all day while one works, leaving a radio or TV on and/or having a playmate for your Terrier is suggested as the Parsons are very social creatures and are prone to anxiety issues in the form of bloody stools, refusal to drink or eat without their owner present, and barking until they lose their voice. The Jack Russell Parson Terrier is not a mean dog and will not attack other animals unless he/she is raised with an iron fist. The dogs are loving, loyal, and make great family pets with people who treat these animals as family members.

SCOTTISH TERRIER

The Scottish Terrier (also known as the Aberdeen Terrier), popularly called the Scottie, is a breed of dog best known for its distinctive profile. It is one of five breeds of terrier that originated in Scotland. The other four are Skye, Cairn, Dandie Dinmont, and West Highland White Terriers. A Scottish Terrier is a small but resilient terrier. Scotties are fast and have a muscular body and neck (a typical neck size is 14 inches), often appearing to be barrel chested. They are short-legged, compact and sturdily built, with a long head in proportion to their size. The Scottie should have large paws adapted for digging. Erect ears and tail are salient features of the breed. Their eyes are small, bright and almond-shaped and dark brown or nearly black in colour. Height at withers for both sexes should be roughly ten inches, and the length of back from withers to tail is roughly eleven inches. Generally a well-balanced Scottie dog should weigh from 19-22 pounds and a bitch from 18-21 pounds. The Scottie typically has a hard, wiry, long, weather-resistant outer coat and a soft dense under coat. The head, ears, tail and back are traditionally trimmed short. Scotties, like most terriers, are alert, quick and feisty — perhaps even more so than other terrier breeds. The breed is known to be independent and self-assured, playful, and intelligent. They are widely considered to be especially loyal by their owners, even as compared with other dogs. Scotties, while being very loving, can also be particularly stubborn. The Scottish terrier makes a good watchdog due to its tendency to bark only when necessary and because it is typically reserved with strangers — although this is not always the case and it is important to remember that all dogs differ. It is a fearless breed that may be aggressive around other dogs unless introduced at an early age. The Scottie is prone to dig as well as chase and hunt small vermin, such as Squirrels, rats, mice and foxes — a trait that they were originally bred for.

WEST HIGHLAND WHITE TERRIER

West Highland White Terriers, commonly known as Westies, are a breed of dog known for their spirited personality and brilliant white coat. They are friendly, good with older children, and thrive on lots of attention. This breed is commonly recognised because it is used as a mascot for Black & White (a brand of Scotch whisky) and for Cesar brand dog food. They have bright, deep-set eyes, as dark as possible, with a penetrating gaze. The ears are small, pointed and erect, giving the animal an alert ready-for-anything look. They typically weigh about 15 to 20 lbs (7.5–10 kg) and their average height is 11 in. (28 cm) at the withers. Their tails, typically naturally "carrot-shaped", should never be docked and are held upright. The tail should be between 5-6 inches. They also have deep chests, muscular limbs, a slightly convex skull, a short and a closely fitted jaw with scissors bite (lower canines locked in front of upper canines, upper incisors locked over lower incisors.) Their teeth generally appear quite large for the size of the dog. Their ears should be held more or less upright, but not pointing straight up; it is essential for any dog to carry themselves properly when showing. Westies have a very strong bone structure for their size. They have a soft, dense undercoat and a rough outer coat, about 2 in.long, that requires regular grooming. Many enthusiasts prefer the "lion cut" where the fur around the face is left long like a lion's mane, but the rest of the fur is cut short. Their paws are slightly webbed, which one can notice by trying to pass their finger between the dog's toes. This breed, descended from working terriers, has a lot of energy, tenacity, and aggression towards its prey, which was originally the rabbit and other smaller animals, such as squirrels. This history has endowed the Westie with a bold temperament that leads many to call them "big dogs in a little body." They are always alert and consider themselves guard dogs, although their size prevents them from providing any real intimidation.

CAVALIER KING CHARLES SPANIELS

Breed standards call for a height between 29 and 33 cm (12-13 inches) with a proportionate weight between 5.5 and 8.5 kg (13 and 18 lbs). Unlike most other spaniels, the Cavalier has a full-length tail well-feathered with long hair, which is typically carried aloft when walking. The breed naturally grows a substantial silky coat of moderate length. Breed standards call for it to be free from curl, with a slight wave permissible. In adulthood, Cavaliers grow lengthy feathering on their ears, chest, legs, feet and tail; breed standards demand this be kept long, with the feathering on the feet cited as a particularly important feature of the breed. A cavalier's coat may be beautiful, but, because it can be long, it is very important to keep it well groomed. The breed is highly affectionate, and some have called the Cavalier King Charles Spaniel "the ultimate lap dog". Most dogs of the breed are playful, extremely patient and eager to please. As such, dogs of the breed are usually good with children and other dogs. This breed is the friendliest of the toy group. For many centuries, small breeds of spaniels have been popular in the United Kingdom. In the eleventh century, in the reign of King Canute, it was illegal to hunt with any dog that could not fit through a gauge that was eleven inches in diameter. Hence, the "birth" of the Toy Spaniel in the United Kingdom. Some centuries later, Toy Spaniels became popular as pets, especially as pets of the royal family. In fact, the King Charles Spaniel was so named because a Blenheim-coated spaniel was the children's pet in the household of Charles I. King Charles II went so far as to issue a decree that the King Charles Spaniel could not be forbidden entrance to any public place, including the Houses of Parliament. Such spaniels can be seen in many paintings of the 16th, 17th and 18th centuries. These early spaniels had longer, pointier snouts and thinner-boned limbs than today's.

CHIHUAHUA

Chihuahuas are best known for their small size, large eyes, and large, erect ears. The AKC (American Kennel Club) recognizes two varieties of Chihuahua: the long-coat and the smooth-coat. Many long-coat Chihuahuas have very thin hair, but other long coats have a very dense, thick coat. Breed standards for this dog do not generally specify a height, only a weight and a description of their overall proportions. As a result, height varies more than within many other breeds. Generally, the height ranges between 6 and 10 inches (15 to 25 cm) at the withers. However, some dogs grow as tall as 12 to 15 inches (30 to 38 cm). AKC show dogs (American standard) must weigh no more than 6.0 lb (2.7 kg). The international FCI standard calls for dogs ideally between 1.5 and 3.0 kg (3.3 to 6.6 lb), although smaller ones are acceptable in the show ring. Chihuahuas are prized for their devotion, ferocity and personality. Their curious nature and small size make them easily adaptable to a variety of environments, including the city and small apartments. Chihuahuas are not well-suited as small children's pets because of their size, temperament and tendency to bite when frightened. Also, many Chihuahuas focus their devotion on one person, becoming overly jealous of that person's human relationships. This can be mitigated through socialization. Chihuahuas seem to have no concept of their own size and may fearlessly confront larger animals, which can result in injury. Because Chihuahuas are such a popular breed, there have been a few clubs made about them. These clubs talk about the breed, host competitions, etc. Sometimes they have information on adoption for members. A couple of clubs are ones such as the Chihuahua Club of America, (CCA) or the British Chihuahua Club. Also, quite a few online forums have been made about these dogs.

MALTESE

The Maltese is a dog belonging to the toy group that is covered from head to foot with a mantle of long, silky, white hair. Adult Maltese range from roughly 3 to 10 lb (1.4 to 4.5 kg), though breed standards, as a whole, call for weights between 4 and 8 lb (1.8 to 3.7 kg). There are variations depending on which standard is being used; many, like the American Kennel Club, call for a weight that is ideally between 4 and 6 lb (1.8 to 2.7 kg), and no more than 7 lb (3.2 kg). The coat is long and silky and lacks an undercoat. The colour is pure white and although cream or light lemon ears are permissible, they are not desirable. Characteristics include slightly rounded skulls, with a one (1) finger width dome. Also, a black nose that is two (2) finger width long. The drop ears with long hair and very dark eyes, surrounded by darker skin pigmentation that is called a "halo", gives Maltese their expressive look. The body is compact with the length equaling the height. Their noses can fade and become pink or light brown in colour. Maltese can be very energetic and are known for their occasional wild outbursts of physical activity, running around in circles chasing their tail, and bolting at top speed with amazing agility. These intelligent dogs learn quickly, and pick up new tricks and behaviours easily. The breed has a reputation for being good-natured, but may be intolerant of small children or other dogs. They can be protective of their owner and will bark or may bite if animals or people infringe on their territory or are perceived as a threat. For all their diminutive size, Maltese seem to be without fear. Maltese have no undercoat, and have little to no shedding if cared for properly. Like their relatives Poodles and Bichon Frisé, they are considered to be largely hypoallergenic and many people who are allergic to dogs may not be allergic to the Maltese. Regular grooming is required to prevent their coats from matting.

POODLE

Poodles are intelligent, active dogs and come in varieties distinguished by size, color, and coat. Toy, miniature, and standard poodles are distinguished by adult shoulder height. Although the FCI lists the country of origin as France, most texts agree that Poodles originated in what is now Germany. Poodles were originally gun dogs and still can be occasionally seen in that role. They are elegant in the show ring, having taken top honors in many shows. The poodle coat is dense and generally does not shed. As a result the coats in showing condition require extensive care and grooming. Most pet Poodle owners keep their Poodles in much simpler cuts that are easier to care for.

According to the AKC standard, a Poodle should be of moderate build, neither heavy or insubstantial. It should have an elegant, balanced appearance, and should carry itself in a "proud" or "dignified" manner. In American Kennel Club (AKC) shows, adults must be shown in the "continental" or "English saddle" clips. Dogs under 12 months old may be shown with a "puppy clip". A handful of registries, such as the United Kennel Club, allow simpler clips. In the puppy clip, the face, throat, base of the tail and feet are shaved. The coat may be shaped with scissors for neatness. In the continental clip the face, throat, feet and part of the tail are shaved. The upper half of the front legs is shaved, leaving "pompoms" around the ankles. The hindquarters are shaved except for pompoms on the lower leg (from the hock to the base of the foot) and optional round areas (sometimes called "rosettes") over the hips. The continental clip is the most popular show clip today. Poodles are intelligent, alert, and active. Poodles are extremely people-oriented dogs and, therefore, are eager to please. They are excellent watchdogs, but unlike some working breeds, don't usually become "one-person" dogs when they are part of a family.

PUG

A Pug is a toy dog breed with a wrinkly face and medium-small body. The word "pug" may have derived from the Latin Pugnus (fist); the Pug's face can look like a clenched fist. Bred to adorn the laps of the Chinese emperors during the Shang dynasty (1766-1122 BC), in East China, where they were known as "Lo-Chiang-Sze" or "Foo". The pug's popularity spread to Tibet, where they were mainly kept by monks, and then went onto Japan, and finally Europe. The breed was first imported in the late 16th and 17th centuries by merchants and crews from the Dutch East Indies Trading Company. The pug later became the official dog of the House of Orange. In 1572, a pug saved the Prince of Orange's life by barking at an assassin. A pug also traveled with William III and Mary II when they left the Netherlands to ascend to the throne of England in 1688. Pugs are very sociable dogs, and usually very stubborn. Yet they are playful, charming and clever and are known to succeed in dog obedience skills. Pugs are sensitive to the tone of a human voice, so harsh punishment is generally unnecessary. In general, they are very attentive dogs, always at their owner's feet, in their lap, or following them from room to room. Because pugs lack longer snouts and prominent skeletal brow ridges, they are susceptible to eye injuries such as puncture wounds and scratched corneas and painful Entropion. Also, the compact nature of their breathing passageways can cause problems such as difficulty breathing. Furthermore, dogs regulate their temperature through evaporation from the tongue. Because of the problems pugs have with breathing, in conjunction with how all dogs regulate their temperature, pugs may have trouble controlling their temperature. Pugs living a mostly sedentary life can be prone to obesity. Therefore, it is important for pug owners to make sure their pets have regular exercise and a healthy diet.

SHIH TZU

The Shih Tzu ("shee tzoo") originated in China. The spelling "Shih Tzu", most commonly used for the breed, is according to the Wade-Giles system of romanization. The Shih Tzu is reported to be the oldest and smallest of the Tibetan holy dogs, its vaguely lion-like look being associated with the Snowlion. It is also often known as the "Xi Shi quan", based on the name of Xi Shi, regarded as the most beautiful woman of ancient China.

The Shih Tzu characterized by its long, flowing double coat; sturdy build; intelligence; and a friendly, lively attitude. In breeding all coat colors are allowed. The Shih Tzu's hair can be styled either in a short summer cut, or kept long as is compulsory for conformation shows.

The American Kennel Club (AKC) Shih Tzu breed standard calls for the dog to have a short snout, large eyes, and a palm-like tail that waves above its torso. The ideal Shih Tzu to some is height at withers 9 to 10 1/2 inches. The dog should stand no less than 8 inches and not more than 11 inches tall. The Shih Tzu should never be so high stationed as to appear leggy, nor so low stationed as to appear dumpy or squatty. Regardless of size or gender, the Shih Tzu should always be solid and compact, and carry good weight and substance for its size range. The American Kennel Club (AKC) American Shih Tzu Club (ASTC) defines the Shih Tzu as a dog that weighs between 9 to 16 pounds as the official breed standard. The life span of a Shih Tzu is 11-14 years, although some variation from this range is possible. The Shih Tzu requires a little more care than some other breeds, and potential owners who are looking for a low maintenance dog should probably choose another breed. Most enjoy a long walk, although they are also quite happy to run around the house.

YORKSHIRE TERRIER

The Yorkshire Terrier, is a breed of small dog in the toy category. The long-haired terrier is known for its playful demeanor and distinctive blue and tan coat. Yorkies can be very small, usually weighing between 5 and 7 pounds (2.5 to 3.5 kilograms). The Yorkie's appearance should be one of spirit, intelligence and vigor. In dog shows, a Yorkie that appears sullen or lifeless will be penalized. Underneath the Yorkie's silky coat, its body is athletic and sturdy, designed for an active life. When trotting about, the Yorkie has a free, jaunty gait, with both head and tail held high. For Yorkies, toy stature does not mean frail or fragile. Yorkshire Terriers are a long-haired breed with no undercoat, which means that they do not shed. Rather, their hair is like human hair in that it grows continuously and falls out rarely (only when brushed or broken). This makes Yorkies one of the best breeds for allergy sufferers. Additionally, since Yorkies carry less dander on their coat, they generally do not have the unpleasant "wet dog" odor when wet. Yorkie puppies are born with a silky-soft black and tan coat and normally have black hairs mixed in with the tan until they are matured. The breed standard for adult Yorkies places prime importance on coat color, quality and texture. The hair must be glossy, fine and silky. From the back of the neck to the base of the tail, the coat should be a dark steel-blue (not silver-blue), never mingled with fawn, bronze or black hairs. Hair on the tail should be a darker blue. On the head, chest and legs, hair should be a bright, rich tan, darker at the roots than in the middle, shading to still lighter tan at the tips. For show purposes, the coat is grown-out long and parted down the middle of the back, but may be trimmed to floor length to give ease of movement and a neater appearance. Hair on the feet and the tips of ears should also be trimmed. The traditional long coat is extremely high maintenance, requiring hours of daily brushing.

BERNESE MOUNTAIN DOG

The Bernese Mountain Dog (also called Berner Sennenhund or Bouvier Bernois) is a versatile breed of farm dog originating in the canton of Berne in Switzerland. A tri-colored dog of large size, the "Berner" (as they are often called) stands 23 to 27.5 inches (58-70 cm) at the withers; breed standards for this breed normally specify no weight, but the usual range is 65 to 120 pounds. The breed is instantly recognized by its distinctive tri-color pattern: body, neck, legs, head and ears are solid black; cheeks, stockings and thumbprints (or ghost eyes) are rust or tan; toes, chest, muzzle, tail tip and blaze between the eyes white. The pattern is rigid and varies only slightly in the amount of white. The eyes are an expressive dark brown and are almond shaped. The Bernese coat is slightly rough in outline, but not at all harsh in texture. The undercoat is fairly dense; the coat is weather resistant. A good brushing every week or two is sufficient to keep it in fine shape, except when the undercoat is being shed; then daily combing is in order for the duration of the moult. The Bernese temperament is a strong point of the breed. Affectionate, loyal, faithful, stable and intelligent but don't forget emotional, Bernese Mountain Dogs make wonderful family pets. The majority of Bernese are very friendly to people, and other dogs. They often get along well with other pets such as cats, horses, etc. The Bernese calm temperament makes them a natural for pulling small carts or wagons, a task they originally performed in Switzerland. With proper training they enjoy giving children rides in a cart or participating in a parade. The Bernese Mountain Dog Club of America offers drafting trials open to all breeds; dogs can earn a NDD (Novice Draft Dog) or an DD (Draft Dog) title. Regional Bernese clubs often offer carting workshops.

BOXER

The Boxer is a breed of stocky, medium-sized, short-haired dog with a smooth fawn or brindled coat and square-jawed muzzle. Boxers have mandibular prognathism, very strong jaws and a powerful bite. They are part of the Molosser group of dogs, bred from the extinct German Bullenbeisser and the English Bulldog. The head is the most distinctive feature of the Boxer. The breed standard dictates that it must be in perfect proportion to his body and above all it must never be too light. In addition a Boxer should be slightly prognathous, i.e., the lower jaw should protrude beyond the upper jaw and bend slightly upwards in what is commonly called an underbite. An adult Boxer typically weighs between 55 and 70 lbs (25 and 32 kg). Adult male Boxers are between 23 and 25 in. (57 and 63 cm) tall at the withers; adult females are between 21 to 23 1/2 in. (53 and 60 cm). Boxers are a bright, energetic and playful breed and tend to be very good with children. Owing to their intelligence and working breed characteristics, training based on the use of corrections often has limited usefulness. Boxers often respond much better to positive reinforcement techniques such as clicker training. It is also true that Boxers have a very long puppyhood and adolescence, and are often called the "Peter Pan" of the dog world. They are not considered fully mature until two to three years of age, one of the longest times in dogdom, and thus need early training to keep their high energy from wearing out their owner. Their suspicion of strangers, alertness, agility, and strength make them formidable guard dogs. They sometimes appear at dog agility or obedience trials and flyball events. These strong and intelligent animals have also been used as service dogs, guide dogs for the blind, therapy dogs, and police dogs in K9 units - a few even herd sheep! The versatility of Boxers was recognized early on by the military, which has used them as valuable messenger dogs, pack carriers, and attack and guard dogs in times of war.

BULLMASTIFF

The Bullmastiff is a powerful dog, said to be a cross between the English Mastiff and the Bulldog. Originally bred to find and immobilise poachers, the breed has proved its value as a family pet. The Bullmastiff is 60% Mastiff and 40% Bulldog and was first recognized in 1924. It is powerfully built and symmetrical, showing great strength, but not cumbersome; it is sound and active. Bullmastiffs are to be 25 to 27 inches at the withers, and 110 to 130 pounds. Females are to be 24 to 26 inches at the withers, and 100 to 120 pounds. Any shade of brindle, fawn, or red is allowed as long as the color is pure and clear. In the United States, however, there is no mention in the standard of the color being "pure and clear". The fawn is a light tan or blond color, while the red is a richer, red-brown. This can range from a deep red to a light red merging with the fawn sometimes described as a red-fawn. A slight white marking on the chest is permissible, but other white markings are undesirable. A black muzzle is essential, toning off towards the eyes, with dark markings around eyes contributing to the expression. The Bullmastiff is courageous, loyal, calm, and loving with those it knows. It has a very strong protective instinct and will defend its owners against anything it perceives as a threat. Rather than attack to protect, it simply knocks the intruder over with its massive size and pins them to the ground, or, will simply stand in front of the stranger/intruder and refuse to let them pass. Bullmastiffs become intensely attached to their families and do best when they can live inside with them. Their protective instinct combined with their great size and natural wariness of strangers means that early socialization is a must. The Bullmastiff may or may not get along well with other dogs. Often, male Bullmastiffs do not tolerate other males, regardless of breed. Occasionally, females are also intolerant of other females. The Bullmastiff, in general, does get along well with children and is very loving towards them.

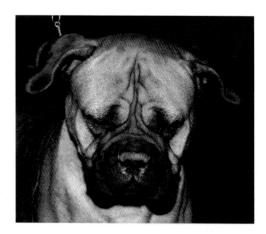

DOBERMAN PINSCHER

The Doberman Pinscher (alternatively spelled Dobermann in many countries) or Doberman is a breed of domestic dog. Doberman Pinschers are known as an intelligent, alert, and loyal companion dog. Although once commonly used as guard dogs, watch dogs, or police dogs, this is less common today. The Doberman Pinscher is a dog of medium size. Although the breed standards vary among kennel and breed clubs, the shoulder height of a Doberman Pinscher bitch is typically somewhere between 24 to 27 inches (61 to 68 cm), and the male typically stands between 26 to 28 inches (66 to 72 cm). The male generally weighs between 75 and 90 pounds and the bitch between 55 and 70 pounds. There is often a slight difference in type between bitches and dogs, with males being decidedly masculine (but not coarse) and females being noticeable feminine (but not spindly). Doberman Pinschers typically have a deep, broad chest, and a powerful, compact, and square muscular body of medium size. The traditional Doberman has always been the one that has had both tail and ears cropped. In some countries, docking and cropping are now illegal, but in some breed shows Doberman Pinschers are allowed to compete with either cropped or uncropped ears. Doberman Pinschers are, in general, a gentle, loyal, loving, and highly intelligent breed. Although there is variation in temperament, a typical pet Doberman attacks only if it believes that it, its property, or its family are in danger. According to the US Centers for Disease Control, the Doberman Pinscher is less frequently involved in attacks on humans resulting in fatalities than several other dog breeds such as pit bull-type dogs, German Shepherd Dogs, Rottweilers and Alaskan Malamutes. Those familiar with the breed consider well-bred and properly socialized Doberman Pinschers to be excellent pets and companions, suitable for families with other dog breeds, excellent with young children, and even cats.

GREAT DANE

The Great Dane is a breed of dog known for its large size and gentle personality. The breed is commonly referred to as the "Gentle Giant". Some sources state that dogs similar to Great Danes were known in Ancient Egypt, Greece and Rome. Various sources report that the Great Dane was developed from the medieval boarhound, and or the Mastiff and Irish wolfhound lines. It is also reported that the Great Dane was developed from mastiff-like dogs taken to Germany by the Alans. The breed may be about 400 years old. The Dane is a true giant among breeds descending from the Mastiff. The Great Dane was developed in Germany to hunt wild boar, and was known as the Boar Hound when it appeared in America late in the 19th century. The Great Dane combines, in its regal appearance, dignity, strength and elegance with great size and a powerful, well-formed, smoothly muscled body. It is one of the giant working breeds, but is unique in that its general conformation must be so well balanced that it never appears clumsy, and shall move with a long reach and powerful drive. . A Great Dane is spirited, courageous, never timid; always friendly and depend-able. This physical and mental combination is the characteristic which gives the Great Dane the majesty possessed by no other breed. It is particularly true of this breed that there is an impression of great masculinity in dogs, as compared to an impression of femininity in bitches. Lack of true Dane breed type, as defined in this standard, is a serious fault. While intimidating in size and stature, this is a breed noted for its gentleness and "human-like" compassion. They make excellent family dogs its impressive size, family devotion and gentle nature combine to create a first-rate companion. The breed also competes well in obedience, agility and tracking. Permissible colors are brindle, blue, black, fawn and the black and whites, harlequin and mantle.

ROTTWEILER

The breed is black with clearly defined tan or mahogany markings on the cheeks, muzzle, chest, legs, and eyebrows. The markings on the chest should form two distinct upside-down triangles, and even a tiny patch of white in between is not acceptable for show dogs. The cheeks should have clearly defined spots that should be separate from the muzzle tan. The muzzle tan should continue over the throat. Each eyebrow should have a spot. Markings on the legs should not be above a third of the leg. On each toe should be a black 'pencil' mark, and the nails are black. Underneath the tail should also be tan. The coat is medium length and consists of a waterproof undercoat and a coarse top coat. Rottweilers tend to be low maintenance, although they experience shedding during certain periods of the year. The skull is typically massive, but without excessive jowls. The forehead may be wrinkly when the Rottweiler is alert, but otherwise the skin should be relatively fitted, or "dry." According to FCI standard, the Rottweiler stands 61 to 68 cm (24-27 inches) at the withers for males, and 56 to 63 cm (22-25 inches) for females. Average weight is 50 kg (110 pounds) for males and 42 kg (95 pounds) for females. In the hands of a responsible owner, a well-trained and socialized Rottweiler can be a reliable, alert dog and a loving companion. In general Rottweilers are fond of children, very devoted, quick to learn, and eager to please. They are typically bright dogs and they thrive on mental stimulation. Rottweilers are playful animals who may frequently demand attention from their owners if they are not receiving the mental stimulation they desire, and they will find creative and often destructive ways to elicit it if they are excessively neglected.

INDEX

HEALTH & Fitness

Healthy
Lifestyles

BY GEMMA McMULLEN

©2017
Book Life
King's Lynn
Norfolk PE30 4LS

ISBN: 978-1-78637-093-8

Written by:
Gemma McMullen

Edited by:
Grace Jones

Designed by:
Natalie Carr

LOOK FOR THE WORDS LIKE **THIS** IN THE GLOSSARY ON PAGE 31.

Contents

DO YOU HAVE ENOUGH VARIETY? FIND OUT INSIDE ON PAGE 12

ARE WE DESIGNED TO EXERCISE? FEATURED ON PAGE 18

HEALTHY

HEALTHY BODY

The way that we treat our bodies is extremely important, because without their good health we would **CEASE** to exist. The food that we eat and the amount that we exercise, both contribute massively to the health of our bodies. We need to respect our bodies in order that they stay healthy for longer.

WHAT IS HEALTHY LIVING?

ALTHOUGH WE ARE ALL UNIQUE, OUR BODIES ALL WORK IN THE SAME WAY AND NEED THE SAME THINGS TO STAY HEALTHY.

HEALTHY living is a term given to the ideal way for us to live our lives; put simply, it means that we live our lives in the healthiest way possible. Healthy living includes the ways that we behave in all aspects of our lives, from the things that we eat to the amount that we sleep.

Living

HEALTHY CHOICES

It is unlikely that we will always choose the healthiest option, but it is important that we have the correct information so we are able to make **INFORMED CHOICES** about the way we live our lives. This book is about exercise and the ways which it contributes to a healthy lifestyle.

HEALTHY MIND

The health of our minds is of equal importance to that of our bodies. Our minds control the way that we think and the ways in which we use our bodies. Keeping a healthy mind includes having healthy relationships with others and being able to deal with our problems rationally.

WHAT IS

HEARTY EXERCISE

EXERCISE is using your body for any activity which makes it work harder than normal. Exercise does not always involve playing sport and does not always make that you feel out of breath and sweaty. If you have done some exercise, your body will feel warm and your heart will beat faster.

A CHILD OF SCHOOL AGE SHOULD EXERCISE FOR ABOUT **ONE HOUR EVERY DAY.**

Exercise?

WHY EXERCISE?

Exercise is good for our bodies and is an important part of a healthy lifestyle. Exercise keeps our hearts and our lungs healthy, and can help to prevent diseases in later life such as heart disease. Exercise also helps to keep our **IMMUNE SYSTEMS** working, so that our bodies are able to fight illnesses such as coughs and colds. Exercise makes our muscles stronger, which means that they can protect the joints in our skeletons. Finally, exercise releases chemicals in our brains called endorphins. Endorphins make us feel happy!

DOING EXERCISE GIVES US A SENSE OF ACHIEVEMENT AND MAKES US FEEL GOOD ABOUT OURSELVES.

DIFFERENT TYPES OF EXERCISE

There are many different types of exercise. Walking to school is a type of exercise, as is walking up the stairs. Team sports involve exercise, as does dancing around in your bedroom to your favourite music. It is important that we exercise every day.

LEVELS OF

1 MILD EXERCISE

Different exercises have different effects on our bodies. Some exercises are mild. They make our hearts beat a little faster and can make us feel warm. Walking is a mild exercise, however, **POWER-WALKING** is classed as a moderate form of exercise.

2 MODERATE EXERCISE

Moderate exercises include activites such as cycling and dancing. Moderate exercises require our bodies to work harder than they normally do. We need to breathe faster when doing moderate exercise and we may start to sweat.

3 VIGOROUS EXERCISE

Vigorous exercise is when we really push our bodies to work as hard as they can. Our hearts, lungs and muscles need to work very hard and we become hot and sweaty. Vigorous exercises include running and playing football.

Exercise

LEVELS OF FITNESS

If our bodies are not used to a lot of exercise, then we will find it difficult to exercise for long periods of time. For example, someone who is not used to running, may only be able to run for two or three minutes. The more that we do exercise, however, the better that our bodies become at it. By exercising regularly, we build up our **STAMINA**, which means that we can exercise for longer.

OUR BODIES NEED TO REGULARLY ATTEMPT ALL LEVELS OF EXERCISE IN ORDER TO STAY HEALTHY.

TYPES OF

TEAM SPORTS

Team sports are a really fun way of exercising, because they are done alongside other people. As well as getting exercise, they provide a good opportunity to have fun with your friends, and even make some new ones. They also allow other players to encourage you on the days that you do not feel like exercising. Most schools play team sports such as football, rugby and netball. If you put in enough practice, you may even make the school's team and play against teams from other schools.

VARIETY OF EXERCISE

OUR bodies need to take part in a variety of exercises, in order to be as healthy as possible. There are so many forms of exercise to choose from and not everybody likes to do the same thing.

Exercise

BENEFITS FOR THE BODY

Different exercises have different benefits for the body. Some improve the strength of our muscles and some improve our stamina. Other exercises are good for our flexibility, helping us to twist and bend. Ideally, we should partake in many different forms of exercise.

WHY NOT SEE IF THERE IS A PARK RUN IN YOUR LOCAL AREA?

SWIMMING IS VERY GOOD FOR OUR BODIES. IT IMPROVES STRENGTH, STAMINA AND FLEXIBILITY **AND IS EASY ON OUR JOINTS TOO.**

GOING SOLO

Not everybody is suited to being part of a team and some people prefer to exercise alone. Running and swimming are both good activities for those people, because they can go at their own pace. **GOING SOLO** doesn't have to be lonely; some people join local running groups where people run at the same time but at their own speed. This too, can be a good way to meet new people.

STAMINA, STRENGTH AND Flexibility

EXERCISE VARIETY

DIFFERENT types of exercise require us to use different parts of our bodies and can effect our fitness in different ways. aerobic exercises improve our stamina, whilst others work on strength and flexibility. It is best if we do a variety of exercises and try to improve all three of these key areas.

STAMINA

Our stamina is our ability to exercise for any length of time. Stamina is most improved through vigorous exercise, such as running or playing tennis. The more regularly that we vigorously exercise the better our bodies will become at lasting for longer before feeling tired.

STRENGTH

Using our muscles helps to make them stronger. Vigorous exercise will improve muscle strength, but there are some far milder exercises that will also do so. Some adults choose to lift weights in order to strengthen their muscles, but that is not safe for children to do. Climbing frames and monkey bars at the park will help to improve muscular strength. You could also do exercises such as sit-ups or push-ups.

FLEXIBILITY

Our flexibility allows us to stretch and bend. The more that we practise, the more flexible that our bodies become. You can increase your flexibility just by stretching more than usual to reach things. Sports which improve flexibility include gymnastics and martial arts.

WHAT HAPPENS TO OUR BODIES DURING
Exercise?

CHANGES TO THE BODY

DEPENDING on the level of the exercise we do, there are significant changes to the body during exercise which help our bodies to cope with the increase in activity. The more we exercise, the more that our bodies will become used to these changes.

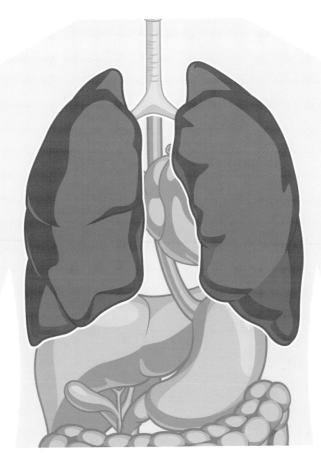

THE LUNGS

The lungs are extremely important because they take in the air that we breathe, including **OXYGEN**. The oxygen is then transferred to our blood. We breathe much faster when we exercise, so our lungs have to work harder. Exercising regularly means that our lungs will become stronger and more flexible.

THE HEART

The heart is the strongest muscle in the human body. It beats constantly and never gets tired. The heart pumps oxygen-carrying blood around the body. When we exercise, the blood needs to move quicker so the heart has to pump faster. It is good for the heart to be exercised regularly to keep it healthy.

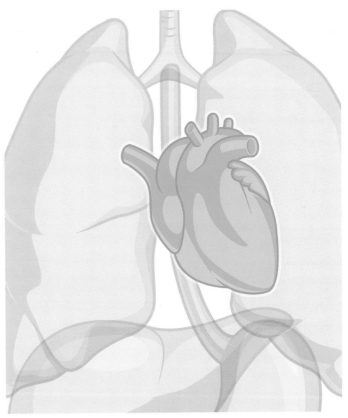

THE HEART AND THE LUNGS

Your heart, lungs and blood make up what is called your **AEROBIC SYSTEM**. Together, they take oxygen in from the air that you breathe and move it around your body. When we exercise, our hearts and our lungs need to work much harder than when we are resting.

When we exercise vigorously, our bodies start to sweat. This is a natural process which happens to everyone. We sweat because it helps to cool our bodies down when they are becoming too warm. We tend to sweat more as we get older, so it is important that we wash ourselves daily.

MUSCLES

MUSCLES cover the bones of our skeletons and allow us to move. Our brains send messages to our muscles when we want to move them. With exercise, our muscles get bigger and stronger, and we are able to do more with them. We must be careful though, as muscles can be damaged during exercise. It is important that we warm them up and cool them down before and after exercise (see page 30).

EVERY BODY IS DIFFERENT

Whilst these changes happen to everyone during exercise, each of our bodies are unique and the effects of exercise are different from person to person. The fitter that we become through exercise, the longer it will take for these changes to occur and the more **SUBTLE** they will become.

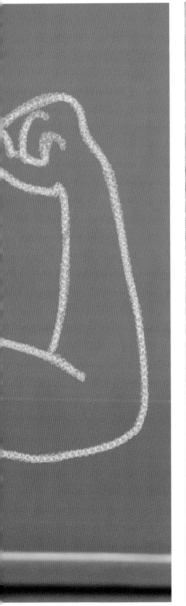

BECOMING FLUSHED

When we exercise, our faces and bodies can become very red. Again, this is a natural process that we are unable to control. This is one of the ways that the body helps itself to cool down. Blood from inside our bodies moves underneath the surface of our skin, in order to cool itself down.

DESIGNED TO

DESIGNED TO EXERCISE

WHILST everyone's body is a little different, every human body needs to exercise, which is why it can become unhealthy if we do not do so. It is actually easier for our bodies to walk for thirty minutes rather than to stand still for the same amount of time – why not give it a try?

Exercise

BORN TO BREATHE

Our hearts, lungs and blood make up our aerobic systems, which give us the ability to breathe and to move oxygen around our bodies. We would not be able to survive without this. Exercise is proven to enhance our hearts and lungs' ability to do their jobs.

BORN TO COMPETE

Whilst not everyone enjoys being competitive, sometimes a level of competition is healthy for us. Our **ANCESTORS** would have had to compete against others while hunting, the quickest and strongest hunter would have been the most successful one.

BORN TO COMPETE

Whilst not everyone enjoys being competitive, a level of competition is healthy for us. Winning a competition can make us feel good and encourage us to work harder. Athletes often compete to win awards.

A CHANGE OF Pace

TECHNOLOGY

NEW technology is always being invented, and is often able to do the jobs that humans used to. This has meant that we are moving our bodies less and less because we are spending more and more time sitting down.

THE CAR

The motor-car was invented in the 1800s, and can now be found in most towns and cities across the world. These days, lots of people own at least one car. Whilst cars are very useful, the more that we use them for shorter journeys, the less we are exercising. Think about this next time you get a lift to school or to a friend's house – could you walk?

HAVING THE BEST OF BOTH WORLDS

It is important to limit the amount of time you spend watching television or playing on the computer. This way you are able to participate in gaming, but will not get lost in a game for hours at a time. Some games are interactive and require you to exercise whilst playing them, such as dancing or bowling. Why not invite a friend round and play an active game together?

GAMING

More and more children are now into gaming, which means that they play computer games. There are many different consoles to choose from and games that are played over the internet too.

Whilst gaming can be enjoyable, it often means that we spend less time with other people, and more time on our own. It is also played indoors and does not allow the body to move much. The more that we game, the less that we exercise.

Exercise

EVERYONE CAN EXERCISE

THERE are so many ways that you can exercise, that everyone can do it. Regular exercise has so many proven benefits, it can even help you to live longer! Studies have shown that moderate exercise for 30 minutes a day can extend your life by a whole year, whilst exercising vigorously for the same time can give you an extra three to four years!

FOR ALL

EXERCISE FOR MENTAL WELL-BEING

A healthy body helps us to have a healthy mind. Exercise makes us feel happier, which improves our **MENTAL STATES**. Being with others during exercise means that we are more likely to have friends and feel good about ourselves. Exercise often means that we are outside getting fresh air too!

EXERCISING WITH A DISABILITY

It may be harder to exercise for a person with a disability, but there are so many options out there that it should never be impossible. The Paralympics are becoming as popular as the Olympics and include athletes with many different disabilities.

EXERCISE FOR FUN

Exercise can be very fun. You don't have to be running marathons or competing in competitions to be getting exercise. Playing games in the park or playground can be fun and exciting ways of moving your body. A game of chase can improve your stamina, practising handstands can improve your strength and simple gymnastics can improve flexibility.

FUEL FOR

BALANCE

O bodies need fuel in order for them to function properly. The fuel that we give our bodies is food. The healthier that we eat, the more likely that it is that we can exercise well. There are five main food groups and it is important that we eat a good balance of each food type. We call this a balanced diet.

CARBOHYDRATES

PROTEIN

SU

FOOD FOR ENERGY

Some foods give us more energy than others. Foods that are high in sugar, such as sweets and fizzy drinks, do give us energy, but the energy comes in short, sharp bursts. If we exercise after eating sugary foods, we won't be able to maintain our energy levels for very long.

Exercise

CARBOHYDRATES

Carbohydrates also contain energy for our bodies, but the energy is released far more slowly, meaning that we are able to exercise for longer periods of time.

Whilst it is still important to eat food from all of the groups, if you know that you are going to be undertaking a lot of exercise, it is good to eat some carbohydrates first.

FRUITS AND VEGETABLES

DAIRY

ATHLETES KEEP UP THEIR ENERGY STORES BY EATING FOODS SUCH AS PASTA AND BANANAS WHICH ARE HIGH IN SLOW-RELEASE ENERGY.

Keeping SAFE

HELMETS

Some types of exercise need safety equipment, and it is important that we equip ourselves accordingly. When riding a bike, for instance, it is **VITAL** that we wear a safety helmet. Falling off a bike without a helmet can be very dangerous. Skateboarders need to wear helmets for the same reason. It is also a good idea to wear knee and shoulder pads when skating, to protect your joints if you should fall.

TAKE A
MOBILE PHONE
WHERE
POSSIBLE
SO THAT
YOU CAN
CALL
SOMEONE
IF YOU GET
INJURED.

GUM SHIELDS

There a some sports where you would need to wear a gum shield. Gum shields are used to protect the teeth. Contact sports, where players touch other players, depend upon gum shields to keep themselves safe. Rugby is a contact sport. Gum shields are also essential when playing hockey, in case a stick accidentally hits somebody in the face.

HARNESSES

Harnesses are used to hold a person's weight. People who take part in climbing wear harnesses in case they slip and fall away from the climbing wall. It is important never to climb without a correctly fitted safety harness. Trampolinists also use harnesses when they are learning a new move or a flip. This stops them from accidentally exiting the trampoline.

THINK SAFE!

Exercise should always be fun, but before undertaking any exercise, think about any potential dangers that you might face. If you are out to exercise alone, make sure that an adult knows where you are.

TOO MUCH

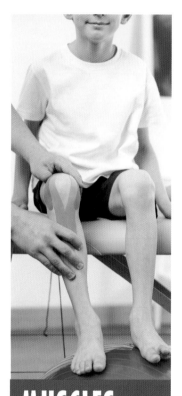

MUSCLES AND JOINTS

Muscles and joints need to be rested, or they will become overworked. Too much exercise can be **DETRIMENTAL** to our bodies, because muscles can be more easily damaged, making them weaker. We are more likely to become injured if we do not allow our bodies to recover after we have exercised, meaning that we will have to rest for longer.

REST AND RECOVER

WHILST everybody needs to exercise, it is important not to exercise too much. Too much exercise can be just as damaging to our bodies as not enough. Bodies need to rest and recover between exercising, or they will become unwell.

Exercise?

LOSING WEIGHT

Alongside healthy eating, exercising can be used as a sensible way of helping a person to lose weight, should they need to. However, too much exercise can cause a person to become underweight, especially if they are not eating a balanced diet. Being underweight puts serious pressure on the body and can make a person unwell.

ENOUGH SLEEP

Exercise aids a good night's sleep, because our bodies feel tired and need to rest. Sleep is extremely important for our development, and a child of primary school age needs at least ten hours each night. Too much exercise, can result in a person not having enough time to get a good night's sleep.

WARMING UP
AND
Cooling Down

WARMING UP

A warm-up routine prepares the body for exercise. By warming your body up properly before exercise, you reduce the likelihood that you will become injured. Warm-ups should start slowly and should include some of the exercises that your body is about to undertake. Stretching muscles and joints during a warm-up will make them more flexible.

COOLING DOWN

A cool-down routine will make it far less likely for you to feel sore following exercise. This routine is a slower version of the exercise achieved and, like the warm-up, should include some stretching. The older that our bodies get, the more they will benefit from warming-up and cooling-down, so it is a good idea to get into the habit of it now.

Glossary

ancestors — persons from whom one is descended, for example a great-grandparent

cease — stop

detrimental — tending to cause harm

going solo — doing something alone

immune systems — the body's defence against illness

informed choices — knowing all the options before you make a choice

mental state — how well your mind is

power-walking — very fast walking

stamina — amount of time we can do something for

subtle — slight

vital — needed

Index

PHOTO CREDITS

Photocredits: Abbreviations: l–left, r–right, b–bottom, t–top, c–centre, m–middle. All images are courtesy of Shutterstock.com.
2 – Sergey Novikov. 3mr – Gladskikh Tatiana. 3br – FamVeld. 4–5m – jordache. 4mr – www.BillionPhotos.com. 4br – Duplass . 5tr – amenic181. 5br – pathdoc. 6r – iofoto. 7r – Zsolt Biczo. 8–9t – Pressmaster. 8–9m – Nataliya Hora. 8–9b – Fotokostic. 9mr – Rawpixel.com. 10–11m – Pressmaster. 10br – Maksim Shmeljov. 11tm – Sergey Novikov. 12bl – Cristian M. 12tr – Gianni Caito. 13bl – Gladskikh Tatiana. 13tr – Vitalinka. 14m – Sergey Novikov. 15t – bluezace. 15b – bluezace. 16tr – Aleksandr Sementinov. 16bl – Robert Kneschke. 17tl – alexkatkov. 17br – Nancy Hixson. 18m – FamVeld. 19tr – Yuliya Evstratenko. 19br – Sergey Novikov. 20m – Rawpixel.com. 20bl – Monkey Business Images. 21tl – Barone Firenze. 21b – Khakimullin Aleksandr. 22m – Monkey Business Images. 23br – Duplass. 23m – rmnoa357. 24ml – Boris Bulychev. 24–25m – ifong. 26m – Kaspars Grinvalds. 27t – Paleka. 27b – wavebreakmedia. 28–29m – Oksana Mizina. 28bl – Photographee.eu. 29mr – Vikulin. 30r – Oksana Kuzmina. 30bl – Tatyana Vyc. 31br – amenic181.
Images are courtesy of Shutterstock.com. With thanks to Getty Images, Thinkstock Photo and iStockphoto.